Aspect of Plant Sciencs Vol. 18

HEAVY METAL POLLUTION AND MYCORRHIZA

Professor G. D. Sharma
Dean, School of Life Sciences
Assam University,
Silchar – 788 011, Assam.

&

Dr. Tali Ajungla
Department of Botany
Nagaland University,
Lumami – 798601, Nagaland.

Today & Tomorrow's Printers and Publishers
4436/7, Ansari Road, Daryaganj, New Delhi - 110 002 (India)
Ph : 23242621; 23241021; Fax 23242621; E-mail: ttpp@vsnl.net

ISBN 81-7019-454-7 (India)
ISBN 1-55528-311-X (USA)

Published by
Today and Tomorrow's Printers and Publishers
4436/7, Ansari Road, Daryaganj, New Delhi - 110 002 (India)
Ph : 23242621; 23241021; Fax 23242621; E-mail: ttpp@vsnl.net

CONTENTS

PREFACE

The heavy metal pollution is a major threat to environmental degradation. These pollutants in soil environment are one of the important factor to the forest decline in various countries. The use of fungicides, pesticides and chemical fertilizers to enhance the yield of agricultural crop is responsible to increase the level of heavy metal contamination of soil. A team of scientists from Sweden has studied the health of soil under different agricultural practices. The team observed that soil contamination exceeded five times higher in metal contaminated soil via manuring, precipitation, leaching and municipal wastes than mixed organic farming which could retain the quality farming for 70 years and 300 years respectively.

The term heavy metal is generally used for a metal having specific gravity greater than about 5, specially when it is poisonous in lower quantity, e.g., lead (Pb), mercury (Hg) etc. The term is also used for the Metals having relatively higher atomic mass and poisonous in higher concentration, e.g., Cu, Zn, etc. A number of sources like industrial effluents, leaded petrol, mining's spoils, foundries, coal burning, are etc. adding the metals to the soil and then into lakes and rivers by acid rain. Anthropogenic activities also alter the heavy metals release to the environment and cause toxicity due to bio-concentration in food chain. Heavy metals cause myriad types of health hazards like reduction of the growth of plants or deaths of various microbes. Cadmium, lead and mercury are of greatest public health concern. The importance of these heavy metals was recongised in 1998 when the United Nation (U.N.) proposed a protocol on long term trans-boundary air pollution on heavy metals.

Microbes are the first organisms to encounter heavy metal pollution. It reduces microbial diversity. Heavy metals also affect various microbial activities and their growth in soil ecosystem. However, the status of heavy metals in soils is affected by different patterns of land use. Soil pollution by heavy metals causes stress for evolutionary genes for resistance. The ecological and physiological alterations due to heavy metals in the plants having mycorrhizal system, a link between polluted soil and roots of higher plants, which helps the plants in absorption, accumulation, detoxifying and increasing resistance in plants against the heavy metals. Therefore, the improved growth and survival of plants on heavy metal contaminated soils by mycorrhiza has been observed in various afforestation programmes. Selection of microbes which can be more beneficial in agriculture and forestry in phytoremediation of heavy metals is the need of present time.

This book is prepared on the experimental study of mycorrhizal system of tree species carried out under various heavy metals pollution. We are quite hopeful that it will be very useful to the Researchers working in the fields of ecology, forestry, agriculture, microbiology and Life Sceinces.

We are deeply indebted to Professor M.N.V. Prasad (Hyderabad), M.S. Dkhar (Shillong), G.K.N. Chettry (Imphal). D.K. Jha (Gauhati), H. Kayang (Shillong), A.K. Shukla (Itanagar), S.C. Tiwari (Raipur), S.C. Srivastava (Agartala), M. Pradhan (Sikkim), C.S. Rao (Shillong), S.R. Joshi (Shillong) for their constructive suggestions. We are obliged to our colleagues Dr. D.Kar, S. Giri, M.D. Choudhury, S.K. Panda, M. Bawri, H. Upadhyay, N.S. Jamir, S.K. Chaturvedi, S.K. Ghosh, B.K. Tiwari, S. Das A. Gupta and A.K. Das for stimulatory discussions on the topics related to Heavy metals pollution in the environment.

G.D. Sharma

Tali Ajungla

Introduction

The term heavy metal is applied to any metallic element that has relatively high density and is toxic at low concentrations, e.g. Hg, Cd, As, Cr, Ti., Pb. etc. Some metals needed in low concentrations but toxic in higher concentrations e.g., Cu, Zn, Se, etc. Metals having more than 5 specific gravity are also generally termed as heavy metals. Heavy metals are toxic to all living organisms if present in environment in higher concentrations. The use of heavy metals is done in various ways like use of fungicides, pesticides, lead pipes, leaded petrol, lead batteries, municipal wastes, mining activities etc. in large scale and polluting the environment. Scientists have been carrying out systematic studies on their effects on plants, animals, fishes, enzymatic processes etc. these studies have lead to a vast literature on this subject. The toxicity of heavy metals studied in laboratory may not be comparable to field studies. To compare relative toxicity of various heavy metals like Cu, Cd, Zn, Ni and Pb varies in forested or non forested soils.

The sensitivity to heavy metals depend on a number of factors e.g. microbial diversity and their degrading capacity of heavy metals, types of soil, water holding capacity of soil, plant diversity, pH, Organic matter, Oxygen content, temperature etc. Heavy metals can enter water supply by industrial wastes or improper waste disposal or by acid rains releasing metals into soils, streams, lakes, rivers and ground water. The most common heavy metal pollutants are mercury, lead and cadmium. Cadmium is used in nickel batteries used in computers, as a corrosion resistant, pigment stabilizer in PVC pipes, in alloys and electronic goods. It is also present as contaminants in fertilizers, detergents and refined petroleum products, cigarettes etc. Long term exposure to cadmium lead to Lung diseases and cancer, renal disfunction, bone defects, increase blood pressure etc. Chromium is used in pigments for paints, cement, paper, rubber which can cause intestinal irritation, cause damage to kidney, liver and nervous system, accumulate in water bodies and becomes dangerous of fish eating which have been exposed to high levels of chromium. Lead poisoning arises from both natural and man made sources. Exposure and level of lead can cause problems in kidneys, or nervous systems, pollutants of lead comes from batteries, petrol additives, alloys, pigments, cable sheathing, ammunition etc. Mercury is a global pollutant as emission from volcanoes and evaporation from natural water bodies and present in the atmosphere as gaseous element. Inorganic mercury poisoning causes tremoring, gingivitis, abortion and congenital malformation. Copper, Nickel and Selenium also cause damage to algae, heart and liver and loss of hair and nervous system respectively. These heavy metals enter into food chain from Water -> Soil -> Plants -> Animals -> Human Food and atmosphere. The important disasters with heavy metals due to Mercury containing sewage contaminating into Minimata Bay in Japan in 1932, 1952, Fish deaths due to mercury poisoning in Sandoz in 1906 and damage to bird sanctuary in Europe and Spain in 1990- 2004 are well documented.

Microbes are the first to be affected by heavy metals in soil or water environments. Their ability to diffuse the pollutants vary and accordingly nutrient cycle and soil fertility (C,N, P, S etc) gets affected. Gram positive bacteria are more sensitive to heavy metals than their counterparts of gram negative ones. In general bacteria are more sensitive than actinomycetes, fungi and algae. However, there is need to study the effects of heavy metals on numbers, sensitivity and resistance in soil microbial community. We may prepare dose response curve for heavy metals and microbial enzyme activities like, co_2 evolution, urease, phosphatase, dehydrogenase, sulphatase or their protein, DNA etc at different concentrations in spatial dispersion.

Mycorrhizal association is ubiquotous symbiotic association with higher plants, which provides a direct link between soil and roots. The absorption of nutrients and their translocation to the plants through this has been investigated. Disversity and distribution of mycorrhiza in native and man made ecosystems have been studied dealing with its ecological and physiological aspects. Heavy metals absorption by various soil compounds and their translocation in Plant-Soil system through mycorrhizal system is insufficiently studied. Role of mycorrhiza in absorption, accumulation, denaturalization and translocation of heavy metals provide a unique area of study to understand their effect on growth, development and productivity of plants.

The book presents a review on various aspects of interactions between heavy metals and ectomycorrhiza an important association between roots of timber yielding trees and fungi. Tolerance of mycorrhiza to heavy metals, enzyme activity, metal uptake and transfer, uptake and accumulation by mycorrhizal system and its transfer to plants have been presented based on the research findings in first five chapters and the possible mechanism involved in metal tolerance in plants in last sixth chapter.

The book will provide an important information on determining the toxicity levels of different heavy metals to mycorrhizal system and its possible role in remediation approach to solve the toxic metal pollution problem in water and soil an important environment pollution threat to the Biosphere. It will also be helpful to evolve strategies for improving the phyto-remediation.

Heavy Metal Pollution and Mycorrhiza : **1-20**
Authors : Prof. G. D. Sharma and Dr. Tali Ajungla
Today & Tomorrow's Printers and Publishers. New Delhi-110 002

Chapter 1

Heavy metal pollution in soil

Introduction

Exposure to high concentration of heavy metals results in reduction of growth in plants. Currently, heavy metals pollution is a serious global environmental issue. As a result of prolonged exposure to plants, certain toxicity symptoms such as chlorosis and necrotic lesions develop. These heavy metals are deposited into the environment through mining activities, industrial discharges, urbanization such as automobile exhaust, fossil fuel combustion etc., excessive use of chemical fertilizers and pesticides and sewage disposal. This atmospheric input of heavy metals can lead to their accumulations in the soil of forest ecosystems, especially of lead and cadmium (Zottl, 1985 and Kahle *et al.*, 1992). Higher concentration of certain metals such as Cu, Pb and Zn act as environmental stress factors, as their influences may bring about physiological reactions in the host plant (Levitt, 1980) resulting in reduction in vigor, growth, reproduction and in extreme, conditions even death.

Heavy metals are among the elements that are not removed or degraded and therefore accumulate in soil or water sediments (Bussotti *et al.*, 1983; Hunter *et al.*, 1987). These heavy metals severly influence the growth and regeneration capacity of forest trees (Wotton *et al.*, 1986; Bell and Teramura., 1991). Excess heavy metals influence both soil properties and rate of litter decomposition (Bond *et al.*, 1986) and they negatively affect seedlings, whose root initially develops in the most contaminated layers (Patterson and Olson, 1983). An increasing accumulation of heavy metals in the upper layer of soil due to atmospheric deposition has been observed even far from sources of emissions (Wotton *et al.*, 1986). At such sites, these heavy metals appear to contribute to the 'new type forest decline' (Heale and Ormrod, 1982; Godbold, 1991). High concentration of dissolved aluminium has resulted in screening of many forest tree species for Al sensitivity (Anderson, 1988 and Shaedle *et al.*, 1989). The heavy metals which are commonly found in soil due to activities of human being include copper, lead, zinc, nickel, cobalt, cadmium, and mercury. Although some of these elements are required in trace amount by living organism for normal physiological process, yet excessive amount is toxic to most living forms. Carlile and Watkinson (1994) concluded that zinc is an essential element required at all concentrations by all fungi. By contrast cadmium and lead are non-essential elements which can be toxic above threshold concentrations (Smith and Read, 1997). This problem of heavy metal toxicity is aggravated further due to their persistence in nature or in the environment. It is therefore, an urgent necessity to deal with this problem created by excess amount of metal already present in the soil.

Metals availability in soil

The acidity in soil increases the metal availability in soil. The hydrogen ion has a higher affinity for negative charges on the colloids thus competing with the metal ions of these sites, thus releasing metals (Greger, 1999). Various factors are known which affect the solubility and availability of metals. This include their chemical characteristics, loading rate, pH, cation exchange capacity (CEC), redox potential, soil texture, clay content and organic matter content (Verloo and Eeckout, 1990).

Due to various human activities the heavy metals are enriched in soil. As a result of these activities, heavy metals are transported to the environment by air and water, thereby increasing the metal concentration in the environment and sediment where they are bound. However, the time taken for them to become bound may be fairly long and it has been shown that the bioavailable fraction of metal in soil is high at the beginning of the binding period but decrease with time (Martin and Kaplan, 1998). Heavy metals when present in soil, they cannot be easily eliminated. Thus a problem arises where availability of heavy metals increases due to human activity.

Uptake of heavy metal by plants

Plants take up heavy metals that are available in soil, air, water and sediment. Mosses accumulate metals from air using their shoot or thallus whereas macroalgae use their thallus to accumulate metals from water (Greger, 1999). The metal that is taken up by plant tissue is then released back into soil, water and air in the gas form mainly from the leaves.

Some elements such as lead has a very short retention time in water, whereas zinc remains longer. Therefore, metals are concentrated in plant tissue depending on different types of the metals in different media (Forstner and Wittman, 1979). Some external forces such as salinity and organic matter also influence the uptake of metal by palnts (Greger and Kautsky, 1993). It is understood that water and air function as transport media and the soil and sediments may be considered as sink for elements, thereby resulting in high concentration of heavy metals.

The movement of metals from the external solution into the cell wall is non-metabolic, passive process driven by diffusion or mass flow (Marschner, 1995). Though the detail mechanism of uptake is not known, however, the uptake of some metal has been reported to be either passive, metabolic/ partially metabolic and partially passive (Cataldo *et al.*, 1983; Bowen, 1987). Costa and Movel (1994) have suggested that 30% of cadmium is taken up passively. When the heavy metals reach the cytoplasm of the plants, they bind the negative charges in various macromolecules of cellular structures. Therefore, the metals remain concentrated in the cytoplasm.

Toxic metals are numerous in their action (Gadd, 1993). In fungi, metal ion can be bound to cell wall polymers such as chitin or melanin and inside the fungal cells they may be rendered harmless to complexation, compartmentation or volatilization. It has been shown that zinc binds to malate and this complex is transported into the vacuole where zinc is released and binds to oxalate, and malate is transported back to the plasma (Mathys, 1977; Harmens *et al.*, 1994). A similar situation is found for cadmium and copper in complexes with phytochelatin (Stiffens, 1990). In this situation, the phytochelatin-Cd complexes enters the plant vacuole and metal is released from the phytochelatin, thus metal may bind into an organic acid in the vacuole.

The uptake level of heavy metal also depends on different plant species. Heavy metals are absorbed by the leaves to different degrees depending upon metal involved (Little, 1973). It is likely that high relative humidity enhances metal uptake through the cuticle in its most open and swollen condition (Greger, 1999). But under low relative humidity the cuticle shrinks and the deposits of epicuticular lipids become compressed, impairing the passage of water soluble metals (Martin and Juniper, 1970).

Accumulation of heavy metals in plants

The heavy metals become concentrated in the tissue due to effluxes and leakages which are likely non-metabolic in action. Atmospheric input of heavy metals can lead to their accumulation in the soil of forest ecosystems especially of Pb and Cd (Zottl, 1985; Kahle *et al.*, 1992). Higher concentration of certain metals such as Cu, Zn and Pb acts as environmental stress factors, as their influences may bring about physiological reactions in the host plant (Levitt, 1980). Zinc is an essential element required at all level of concentration by all fungi (Carlile and Watkinson, 1994). By contrast, Cd and Pb are non-essential elements which can be toxic above threshold concentration (Smith and Read, 1997). The translocation and accumulation of heavy metals may be concentrated in the tissue.

In our study, the response of ectomycorrhizal fungi to heavy metals widely varied which was specific to particular ectomycorrhizal fungal species and the level of metal concentrations. Metal content in non-mycorrhizal root was higher than those of non-mycorrhizal roots. This has suggested that the production of dense mycelium was an advantage for the seedlings by reducing the uptake of added metals. However, once saturation point was reached in the mycelium, the uptake of metals in the plants also increased. The rapid mycelial turn over was associated with metal exclusion and hence avoidance of toxicity. This hypothesis was supported by Colpaert and Van Assche (1992) for Ni and Zn tolerance in plants.

Results have indicated that Cd and Pb were most toxic to ectomycorrhizal fungi. The development of these fungi was inhibited in a moderately contaminated soil. The accumulation of metals in the mycelium and protecting root against metal toxicity was an important factor. Jones and Hutchinsons, (1988) have demonstrated that *Lactarius rufus* increased the Ni tolerance of its host plant for a short time. It is very unlikely that mycorrhizal fungi directly influence the transport of heavy metals in the plants. However, they could influence the amount of metals transported to the roots. All the four ectomycorrhizal fungi studied (*Scleroderma aurantium, Suillus luteus, Cenococcum graniforme,* and *Boletus* sp) had ameliorating effect on the reduction of metal concentration in the root tissue. This has suggested that the whole biomass in sporophore, the extrametrical mycelium and fungal sheath (mantle) can accumulate a considerable amount of heavy metals and thus strongly reduce the availability of the toxic ions to the host. High accumulation of Zn and Cu comparing to Ni, Cd, Pb and Al suggested that Zn and Cu are essential trace elements and are not toxic to the plants and fungal symbiont at lower concentrations. Seedlings root contained high concentration of Cu which is an essential micronutrient for plants and mycorrhizae are proved to sequester it in high quantities (Berthelson *et al.,* 1995). This sequestration could prevent the deleterious effect of heavy metals to the host to a certain extent. Denny and Wilkins (1987) also argued that the extrametrical mycelium played a key role in retention of high amount of Zn ions. Lindsay (1972) also observed high concentration of zinc in root tissue. The metals primarily acted on the mycelium, the fungal tissue might also provide the host with protection against heavy metals depending upon metal accumulation capacity of the mycelium. The influence of metal uptake is presumed to be the greatest for elements which have narrow diffusion zones around the plant root such as cadmium, lead and nickel (Harley and Smith, 1983). In this study, differential metal uptake may be associated with the development of fungal mantle. Bradley *et al.* (1981) also confirmed binding of metals to roots or fungal structures. The relatively high tissue contents of heavy metals in non-mycorrhizal and low amount of Zn, Ni, Cd, Pb, Cu and Al supports this hypothesis.

In trees, the heavy metal concentration in bark is generally found to be higher than in the wood of the stem (Greger and Landberg, 1995). The concentration of metal may be higher in roots than in shoots, since the metals bound largely on the cell walls during uptake. Interestingly, Ajungla and Sharma

(2003) also found high concentration of Cu and Ni in root tissue of *Pinus kesiya* seedlings. (Table 1.1). Studies have been conducted to evaluate the accumulation of cadmium and chelation of metal ions occurring in vicinity of plant roots (Naidu and Harder, 1998). This accumulation of metal pollutants in the plant surface is a contributing factor to the forest decline. Various atmospheric input of heavy metal and mobilization of metals in soil plant system (Srivastava *et al.*, 1999b) can lead to their accumulation in the soil of forest ecosystem. Therefore, a better understanding of heavy metal sources, their accumulation in soil and their effect on plant systems seems to be a particularly important issue of present day research (Rodes *et al.*, 1980).

Heavy metal tolerance in plants

In our study, the accumulation of heavy metal was more in non-mycorrhizal roots than in ectomycorrhizal roots. Significant variation in the metal concentration between various mycobionts (Table 1.2) was observed. The toxic metals are often prevented from interfering with metabolic activities of the host. Greger (1999) concluded that the mechanism behind tolerance involve exclusion of metals or accumulation, including detoxification by trapping, binding or complexation in the tissue. The ability to sequester heavy metals in organs or sub-cellular compartments with little or no sensitive metabolic activity is considered by a key factor in the tolerance of heavy metals (Ernst, 1992; Wang and Evangelou, 1995),

The rhizosphere plays an important role to reduce the metal uptake by increasing pH in the rhizosphere region, thereby, leading to decrease mobility of the metals. The Cu tolerant *Silene cucubalus* excretes a substance to rhizosphere which binds Cu and prevents uptake (Jackson *et al.*, 1990). Some plants develop certain barrier to avoid uptake, but when metal concentration increases, the metal uptake also increases. This may be due to the toxic nature of metals which is present in high amount, thereby, losing the function of barrier for uptake. There are also some types of plants which have ability to detoxify the high amount of metals within the tissue. At high external metal concentrations, however, these plants do not increase their uptake, probably due to competition between metal ions at the site of uptake (Greger, 1999). The metal tolerant plants are usually efficient in avoiding the occurrence of toxic concentration of free heavy metal cations in plasmatic compartments and thereby, avoid the development of oxidative stress (Woolhouse, 1983). When plants are exposed to high concentration of heavy metals without nutritional functions, most plants eventually fail to maintain metals homoeostasis and develop stress symptoms (Dietz *et al.*, 1999). The sequestration of metals seems to be an important tolerance mechanism in plants.

Remediation of heavy metal in polluted soil.

The soil may require remediation if the concentration of heavy metal is in excess. The role of terrestrial plants in remediation of metals polluted soil has been studied by various scientists. Comprehensive reviews of the emerging phytoremediation technologies and the underlying fundamental process are available (Cunningham and Ow, 1996; Entry *et al.*, 1996; McGrath, 1998; Wenzel *et al.*, 1999). Moreover a multitude of remediation technologies has been developed for the clean-up-heavy-metal polluted soils (Iskander and Adriano, 1997; Pierzynshi, 1997).

The concept of phytoremediation is mainly based on the utilization of solar energy through the activity of photosynthesis and transpiration. The utilization of green plants in remediation of contaminated soils, waste and water can play a major role in achieving the goal through indigenous process and as a catalyst in enhancing other natural processes such as microbial activities at lower financial and technical input (Chaney, 1983; Cunninghum and Berti, 1993; Raskin *et al.*, 1994; Wenzel *et al.*, 1999). Five fundamental processes by which plants can be used to remediate contaminated soils, sediments and water have been identified by Wenzel *et al.*, (1999). Phytostabilization is a containment process using pollutant tolerant plants to mechanically stabilize polluted soils to prevent bulk, erosion and airborne transport to other environments. Both agricultural and horticultural crops have shown potential in this approach. Phytoimmobilization processes prevent movement and transport of dissolved contaminants using plants to decrease the mobility of pollutants in soils. Phytoextraction removes both metallic and organic constituents from soil by direct uptake into plants and translocation to above ground biomass. Through this method metals like Pb, Cd Ni, Cr, Cu and V can be removed. Plants such as Brassicae sp are envolved. Phytodegradation results in uptake and plant internal degradation of organic contaminants. They also assist in phytostimulation which stimulate microbial degradation of organic contaminants in the rhizosphere (Walton and Anderson, 1990; Anderson *et al.*, 1992; Cunningham *et al.*, 1995). Phytovolatilization process involved specialized enzymes that can transform, degrade and finally volatilize contaminants in the plant-microbe-soil system (Terry *et al.*, 1992; Schnoor *et al.*, 1995; Terry, 1995; Rugh, 1996). Through this method metals like Hg and Se can be removed from contaminated soils.

The phytoremediation is economically and ecologically friendly which can be used as an alternative method to the conventional remediation technologies. Through this technique, plants can be used to cleanse soil and water. Plants play an important role to accumulate, absorb, detoxify the toxic contaminants present in the environment.

The use of plants for remediation of heavy metals contaminated soils has many advantages as concluded by Saxena *et al.* (1999). Possibility for large scale application is that the plants can be planted in large areas without costing much. Apart from this, plants provide aesthetic value on the contaminated sites. This phytoremediation technology is ecologically and environmentally friendly. The plant species used for phytoremediation can have high economic return which will compensate the cost of technology. The plants also accumulate the pollutants within their tissues, thereby, reducing the ill-effects. Besides this, plants also provide indirect advantages, such as better soil aeration which helps microbial degradation of organic contaminants and microbe-assisted uptake of metals pollutants. It also reduces soil erosion due to plant stand and enhances rhizospheric microflora and fauna thereby maintaining a healthy ecosystem.

The high level of metabolic activity found in roots and shoots of plants may be utilized to aid in the successful phytoremediation of organic contaminants (Schnoor *et al.*, 1995). It is important to identify the plant species which have ability to grow on contaminated sites and also play beneficial role in remediation process.

Rhizosphere microorganisms in contaminated soil.

The term rhizosphere was first coined by Hiltner (1904) to denote the area of intense microbiological activity which extends several millimeter from the root system of the plants. The rhizosphere is considered a unique habitat for microorganisms. The rhizosphere microorganisms differs both quantatively and qualitatively, which differs from plant to plant. The rhizosphere is a zone of increased microbial community which is influenced by root itself. This microbial community of rhizosphere have either beneficial or harmfull effects on the development of plant. The microorganisms colonise the root to utilize the root exudates as food and in turn release exudates from their own cells. There is increasing evidence that rhizosphere processes influenced the plant metal interaction. It is noted that dissolved root exudates increase the solubility of the metals in the rhizosphere depending on the plant species and cultivars (Kauai *et al.*, 1988; Jolly and Brown, 1989; Romheld and Marschner, 1990).

The role of rhizosphere in reducing the mobility of certain pollutants in soil is known. The plants that have more dense and deeper roots are critical to application in any phytoremediation programme. Strategies to enhance root-rhizosphere associations including mycorrhizae have been reviewed by many authors (Stomp *et al.*, 1994; Cunningham *et al.*,1996;

Entry *et al.*, 1996). The distribution of Si, Fe and Mn in the rice rhizosphere of paddy soil was investigated by Lao *et al.*, (1993). They identified a particular zone of accumulation and depletion across the rhizosphere due to interaction between roots and soil processes. Ectomycorrhizal pine seedlings significantly enhance the remediation of heavy metals than mycorrhizal one (table 2). The remediation may reach up to several times in highly polluted soils (table1). The extra mycelium fungal sheath and Hartig net accumulate the pollutants in fungal tissue and detoxify their effect. However, it remains unclear whether fungal tissue can work as sink and then transport to the plants and dilute the concentration in the plant tissue.

Table 1.1 : Concentration of heavy metals (ppm) in the root tissue of mycorrhizal and non-mycorrhizal roots

Element concentration (ppm) in soil	Concentration of heavy metals in different mycorrhizal roots				
	M1	M2	M3	M4	Control
Zn 10	3.4	2.4	2.4	3.0	5.0
Zn 50	24.5	23.7	25.0	20.0	35.0
Zn 100	42.0	39.0	37.0	40.0	45.0
Zn 200	47.0	61.0	55.0	62.0	67.0
Zn 500	95.0	69.0	75.0	85.0	97.0
Ni 10	2.0	2.0	2.0	2.0	3.0
Ni 50	8.0	12.0	13.0	10.0	15.0
Ni 100	22.0	21.0	20.0	30.0	35.0
Ni 200	32.0	29.0	35.0	41.0	44.0
Ni 500	47.0	47.0	40.0	48.0	57.0
Al 10	2.9	2.4	2.1	2.8	5.2

Al 50	3.4	3.5	4.5	5.2	12.0
Al 100	20.0	14.0	13.0	18.0	28.0
Al 200	28.0	28.0	31.0	29.0	35.5
Al 500	52.0	52.0	43.0	40.0	55.0
Cd 10	2.0	1.0	1.0	1.0	3.0
Cd 50	3.0	3.0	2.0	2.0	4.0
Cd 100	7.0	7.0	5.4	4.9	8.1
Cd 200	15.0	9.0	8.3	8.3	15.8
Cd 500	20.0	21.0	17.0	12.0	30.0
Cu 10	5.1	5.8	5.3	4.9	6.1
Cu 50	19.0	10.0	21.0	13.0	27.0
Cu 100	30.0	24.0	23.0	21.0	37.0
Cu 200	39.0	26.0	27.0	26.0	45.0
Cu 500	61.0	45.0	45.0	40.0	85.0
Pb 10	1.6	1.6	1.5	1.4	2.1
Pb 50	2.0	4.0	4.0	2.9	7.0
Pb 100	4.5	10.0	10.0	8.0	12.0
Pb 200	14.0	15.0	15.0	17.0	20.0
Pb 500	30.0	20.0	22.0	20.0	38.0

M1 = *Scleroderma aurantium*, M2 = *Boletus* sp, M3 = *Cenoccocum graniforme*, M4 = *Suillus luteus*

Table 1.2. Analysis of variance (F) of various mycobionts and mycorrhizal and non- mycorrhizal with metal concentration and mycorrhizal infection.

Source of variation	Variation between Various mycobionts	Variation between mycorrhizal and non-mycorrhizal root tissue
Metal concentration	NS	7.61*
Mycorrhizal infection	4.22**	4.5*

* = Significant at p< 0.01 level, ** = Significant at p< 0.05 level

References :

1. Ajungla, T. and Sharma, G.D. 2003. Accumulation of Cu and Ni in ectomycorrhizae of *Pinus kesiya* (Royle ex Gordon). Nagaland University Research Journal. (1):14-17.

2. Anderson, M. 1988. Toxicity and tolerance of aluminium in vascular plants. Water Air Soil Pollution. 39:439-462.

3. Anderson, B., Satler, A., Virgin, I. and Styring, S. 1992. Photodamage of Photosystem II. Primary and secondary events. J. Photochem Photobiol. B. 15:15-31.

4. Bell, R and Teramura, A. H. 1991. Soil metal effects on the germination and survival of *Quercus alba* L and *Q. prinus* L. Environ. Exp. Bot. 31: 145-152.

5. Berthelson, B. O., Olsen, R. A. and Steinnes, E. 1995. Ectomycorrhizal heavy metal accumulation as a contributing factor to heavy metal level in organic surfaces soils. Sci. Total Environ. 170: 141-149.

6. Bond, H., Lihgthart, B., Shimabuku, R. and Russel, L. 1976. Some effects of cadmium on coniferous forest soil and litter microcosm. Soil Sci. 121 (5): 278-187.

7. Bowen, J. E. 1987. Physiology of genotyping differences in zinc and copper uptake in rice and tomato plant. Plant Soil. 99:115-125.

8. Bussotti, F., Rinallo, C., Grossoni, P., Gellini, R., Patani, F. and Delpanta, S. 1983. Degrado della egeta zione costiera nella Tenuta di S. Rossore, La Provincia Pisana. Spec. parco. Nat. igliarino S. Rossore Massaciuccoli e aree protette. 9: 47-52.

9. Cataldo, D.E., Garland, T. R and Wildung, R. E. 1978. cadmium uptake kinetics in intake soyabean plants. Plant Physiol. 73: 844-848.

10. Carlile, M. J. and Watkinson, S. C. 1994. The fungi. Academic Press Ltd., London.

11. Chaney, R. L. 1983. Plant uptake of inorganic waste constituents. In: Pavv J.F., Marsh P.B., Kla J.M. (eds) Land treatment of hazardous wastes. Noyes Data Corp. Park Ridge. N. J. 50-76.

12. Colpaert, J. V. and Van Assche, J. A. 1992. The effect of Cd and Cd-Zn interaction on the axenic growth of ectomycorrhizal fungi. Plant and Soil. 145:237-243.

13. Costa, G. and Novel, J. L. 1994. Water Relations, gas exchange and amino acid content in Cu-treated lettuce. Plant Physiol Biochem. 32: 561-570.

14. Cunninghum, S. D. and Berti, W. R. 1993. remediation of contaminated soils with green plants; An overview. In vitro Cell Dev Biol. 29: 207-212.

15. Cunninghum, S. D. and Lee, C. R. 1995. Phytoremediation: Plant-based remediation of contaminated soils and sediments. Bioremediation: Science and Application. SSSA Special Publication. 43.

16. Cunninghum, S. D. and Ow, D. W. 1996. Promises and prospects of phytoremediation. Plant Physiol. 110:715-719.

17. Denny, S. J. and Wilkins, D. A. 1987. Zn tolerance in Betula sp variation in response to Zn among ectomycorrhizal associates. New Phytol. 106:535-544.

18. Dietz, K. J. and Hartuns, W. 1996. The leaf epidermis: its ecophysiological significance. Prog Bot. 57:32-53.

19. Entry, J. A., Vance, N. C., Hamilton, M. A., Zabowski, D., Watrud, L. S. and Adriano, D. C. 1996. Phytoremediation of soil contaminated with low concentrations of radionucliedes. Water Air Soil Pollut. 88: 167-176.

20. Ernst, W. H. O. 1992. Metal tolerance in plants. Acta Bot Neerl. 41:229-248.

21. Forstner, U. and Wittmann, G. T. W. (eds) 1979. Metal pollution in the aquatic environment. Springer, Berlin, Heidgelberg, New York.

22. Gadd, G. N. 1993. Interactions of fungi with toxic metals. New Phytol. 124: 25-60.

23. Godbold., D. L. 1991. Die wirkung von Aluminium und schwermetallen auf *Picea abies* Samlinge. Sauerlanders, Frankfurt.

24. Greger, M. and Kautsky, L. 1993. Use of macrophytes for mapping bioavailable heavy metals in shallow coastal areas.

Stolckholm, Sweden. Appl. Geochem Suppl. 2:37-43.

25. Greger, M. and Landberg, T. 1995. Cadmium accumulation in *Salix* in relation to cadmium concentration in the soil. Report from Vattenfall Utveckling AB 1995/9 (in Swedish).

26. Greger, M. 1999. Metal availability and bioconcentration in plants. Heavy metal stress in plants: from molecules to ecosystems. Prasad, M. N. V and Hagemeyer, J (eds). 1-27.

27. Harley, J. L. and Smith, S. E. 1983. Mycorrhizal Symbiosis. Academic Press London.

28. Harmens, H., Koevoets, P. L. M., Verkleij, J. A. C. and Ernst, W. H. O. 1994. The role of low molecular weight organic acids in mechanisms of increased zinc tolerance in *Silene vulgaris* (Moench) Garcke. New Phytol. 126:615-621.

29. Heale, E. L. and Ormrod, D. P. 1982. Effects of copper and nickel on *Acer rubrum, Cornus stolonefira, Lonicera tatarica* and *Pinus resinosa*. Can J Bot. 60:2674-2681.

30. Jones, M. D. and Hutchinsons, T. C. 1988. Nickel toxicity in mycorrhizal birch seedlings infected with *Lactarius rufus* or *Scleroderma flavidum*, effect on growth, photosynthesis, respiration and transpiration. New Phytol. 108: 451-459.

31. Hunter, B. A., Johnson, M. S. and Thompson, D. J. 1987. Ecotoxicology of copper and cadmium in a contaminated grassland ecosystem. 1. Soil and Vegetation contamination. J Appl. Ecol. 24: 573-586.

32. Iskander, I. K. and Adriano, D. C. 1997. Remediation of soil contaminated with metals- a review of current practices in the USA. In: Iskander I.K., Adriano D.C. (eds) Remediation of soils contaminated with metals. Science Reviews. Northwood, U. K.

33. Jackson, P. J., Unkerfer, P. J., Delhaize, E. and Robinson, N. J. 1990. Mechanism of trace element tolerance in plants. In: Katterman F (ed). Environmental injury to plants. Acad Pr. San Diego, New York, Boston. 231-255.

34. Jolley, V. D. and Brown, J. C. 1989. Iron efficient and inefficient oats. 1. differences in phytosiderophores release. J Plant Nutr. 12: 423-435.

35. Kahle, H. and Breckle, S. W. 1992. Bleiund Cadmium-Zietbombe in unseren Waldboden. Biologie in Unserer Ziet. 22: 21-27.

36. Kawai, S., Takaji, S. and Sato, Y. 1988. Mugineic acid family phytosiderophores in root-secretions of barley, corn and sorghum varieties. J. Plant Nutri. 11: 633-642.

37. Levitt, J. 1990. Response of plants to environmental stresses 2 second edition. Academic Press, New York.

38. Little, P. 1973. A study of heavy metal contamination of leaf surfaces. Environ Pollut. 5: 159-172.

39. Lindsay, W. L. 1972. Zn in soil and plant nutrition. Adv. Agron. 24; 147-186.

40. Marschner, H. 1995. Mineral nutrition of higher plants. Academic Press, Cambridge.

41. Martin, H. W. and Kaplan, D. I. 1998. Temporal changes in cadmium, thallium and vanadium mobility in soil and phytoavailabiltiy under field conditions. Water Air Soil Pollut. 101: 399-410.

42. Martin, T. J. and Juniper, E. B. 1970. The cuticles of plants. Edward Arnolds, Edinbergh.

43. Mathys, W. 1977. The role of malate, oxalate and mustard oil glucosides in the evolution of zinc-resistance in herbage plants. Physiol Plant. 40: 130-136.

44. McGrath, S. P. 1988. Phytoextraction for soil remediation. In: Brooks RR (ed) Plant that hyper accumulate heavy metals. CAB. International, Wallingford. 261-287.

45. Naidu, R and Harter, R. D. 1998. Effcet of different organic ligands on cadmium absorption by the extractability from soils. Soil Science Society of American Journal. 62(3): 644-650.

46. Patterson, W. A. and Olson, J. J. 1993. Effects of heavy metals on radicle growth of selected woody species germinated on filter paper, mineral and organic soil substrates. Can. J. For. Res. 13: 233-238.

47. Pierzynski, G. M. 1997. Strategies for remediation of trace-element contaminated sites. In: Iskandar, I.K. and Adriano, D.C. Remediation of soil contaminated with metals. Science

Reviews, Northwood, U.K.

48. Raskin, I., Kumar, P.B.A.N., Dushinkow, S. and Salt, D. E. 1994. Bioconcentration of heavy metals by plants. Current opinion in Biotechnology. 5: 285-290.

49. Rhodes, L. H. and Gerdemann, J. W. 1980. Cellular interactions in symbiosis and parasitism. (C.B. Cook, P.W. Pappas and E.D. Rudolp. eds.) The Ohio Stae University Press. Columbus. 173.

50. Romheld, R. and Marschner, H. 1990. Genotypical differences among graminacious species in release of phytosiderophores and uptake of iron phytosiderophores. Plant Soil. 123: 147-153.

51. Rugh, C. L., Wilde, H. D., Stack, N. M., Thompson, D. M., Summers, A. O. and Meager, R. B. 1996. Mercuric ion reduction and resistance in transgenic *Arabidopsis thaliana* plants expressing a modified bacterial Mer A gene. Proct. Natl. Acad. Sci. USA. 93: 3182-3187.

52. Saxena, P. K., Krishnaraj, S., Tan, T., Perras, M. R and Vettakkoromakankav, N. N. 1999. Phytoremediation of heavy metals contaminated and polluted soil. In: Heavy metal stress in plants. From molecules to ecosystem. Prasad MNV and Hagemeyer (eds). 305-329, Kluwer Academic Publ. Dordreaht, The Netherland.

53. Schnoor, J. L., L.A., Licht, S. C., McCutcheon, N.L., Wolfe, L.H. and Carreira. 1995. Phytoremediation of organic and nutrient contaminants. Environ Sci Technol. 29: 318-323.

54. Smith. S. E. and Read, D. J. 1997. Mycorrhizal Symbiosis. 2nd Ed., Academic Press Ltd., London.

55. Srivastava, S. E., Prakash, S and Srivastava, M. M. 1999. Chromium mobilization and plant availability, the impact of organic complexation ligands. Plant Soil. 212: 203-208.

56. Steffens, J. C. 1990. The heavy metal-binding peptides. Annu Rev. Plant Physiol. Plant Molec Biol. 41: 553-575.

57. Stomp, A. M., Han, K. H., Wilbert, S., Gordon, M. P. and Cunningham, S. D. 1994. Genetic strategies for enhancing phytoremediation. Ann NY Acad. Sci. 721: 481-492.

58. Terry, N., Carlson, C., Raab, T. K. and Zayed, A. M. 1992. Rates of selenium volatilization among crop species. J. Environ Qual. 21: 341-344.

59. Terry, N. 1995. Can plant solve the Se problem. In: Abstract book of the fourteenth annual symposium on current topics in plant biochemistry, physiology and molecular biology. University of Missouri. 63-64.

60. Verloo, M and Eeckout, M. 1990. Metal species transformations in soil: an analytical approach. Intern J Environ Anal Chem. 39: 179-186.

61. Walton, B. and Anderson, T. A. 1990. Microbial degradation of trichloroethylene in the rhizosphere. Potential application to biological remediation of waste sites. Appl. Environ Microb. 56: 1012-1016.

62. Wenzel, W. W., Salt, D., Smith, R and Adriano, D. C. 1999. Phytoremediation a plant-microbe based remediation system. In: Adriano D.C., Bollag J.M., Frankenberger W., Sims R. (eds). Bioremediation of contaminated soils. SSSA Special Monograph (In press).

63. Woolhouse, H. W. 1983. Toxicity and tolerance in the response of plants to metals. In: Lange O., Nobel P.S., Osmond C.B., Zieger, H. (eds) Encyclopedia of Plant Physiol, new series vol. 12. Springer, Berlin, Heidelberg, New York. 245-300.

64. Wang, J. and Evangelou, V. P. 1995. Metal tolerance aspects of plant cell wall and vacuole. In : Pessarakli M (ed) Handbook of plant and crop physiology. Dekker, New York. 695-717.

65. Wolton, D. L., Jones, D. C. and Phillips, S. F. 1986. The effect of nickel and copper deposition from a mining and smelting complex on coniferous regeneration in the boreal forest of Northern Manitoba. Water Air Soil Pollut. 31: 349-358.

66. Zottl, H. W. 1985. Heavy metal levels and cycling in forest ecosystems. Experientia. 41:1104-1113.

Heavy Metal Pollution and Mycorrhiza : **21-41**
Authors : Prof. G. D. Sharma and Dr. Tali Ajungla
Today & Tomorrow's Printers and Publishers. New Delhi-110 002

Chapter 2

Heavy metals toxicity in ectomycorrhizal system

Mycorrhizae:

There are few mutually beneficial associations between different organisms. Such as those between alga and fungus in case of lichen, alga and coelenterate in corals, bacteria and plant in nitrogen fixing symbiosis and fungus and roots of higher plants in mycorrhizal associations. The mycorrhizal symbioses are now considered being most common of the symbiotic spectrum. The association is often classified as biotrophic or necrotrophic depending on whether both symbionts remain alive or dead. These two associations however, vary in their physiological functions under different environmental conditions.

Most of the world's terrestrial ecosystems are dominated by plants that require symbiotic association with mycorrhizal fungi to achieve the optimum productivity. Such mutualistic symbiotic association has been recognized for more than a century. Recently, different methods have been developed to employ them in forestry and agriculture. The present scantiness of understanding of the complex array of interactions, mechanisms and strategies retard optimal use of mycorrhizae in efforts to improve forest productivity. The physical and chemical characteristics of the soil influence both the fungus and the host plant roots in establishing the mycorrhizal associations. More information needs to be gathered about ecology and physiology of different mycorrhizal fungi to better predict where and when a specific fungus-host combination is likely to meet the objective of each mycorrhizal management programme.

Types of mycorrhizae:

Mycorrhiza is a universal plant fungal symbiosis. This kind of symbiotic association is always underground. Mycorrhizae represent the least understood but most widespread in the ecosystem. Mycorrhizal associations are diverse in both structure and in their function. Based on anatomical and morphological features, mycorrhizae are divided into three broad groups: ectomycorrhiza, endomycorrhiza and ectendomycorrhiza which correspond to the older terms which were commonly used such as ectotrophic, endotrophic and ectendotrophic mycorrhizae.

Table 2.1: Mycorrhizal types, their characters and distribution within the plant kingdom (after Marks, 1991).

Mycorrhiza	Host range	types of relationships
1. Ectomycorrhiza	Gymnosperms and Angiosperms	Sheath, intercellular hyphae Hartig net, morphological changes in roots
2. Ectendomy-	Gymnosperms and	Sheath optimal, inter &

	corrhiza	Angiosperms Hartig	intra-cellular hyphae, net
3.	Vesicular-Arbuscular Mycorrhiza (VAM)/ Arbuscular Mycorrhizae (AM)	All groups of plant kingdom	Intracellular hyphae vesicle and arbuscle present/vesicles are absent in AM type
4.	Arbutoid mycorrhiza	Very restricted Ericales	Sheath inter-and pelton intra-cellular hyphae
5.	Monotropoid Mycorrhiza	Very restricted monotropaceae	Sheath inter-and coiled intra-cellular hyphae, Hartig net
6.	Ericoid mycorrhiza	Very restricted Ericales	No sheath, no intercellular hyphae, Intercellular
7.	Orchid mycorrhiza	Very restricted orchidaceae	Intracellular coiled hyphae.

Ectomycorrhiza:

Ectomycorrhizae are characteristics of woody perennials in families such as Betulaceae, Fagaceae, Dipterocarpaceae, Myrtaceae, Pinaceae, Juglandaceae and Salicaceae. These families accounts for much of world's wood production. There are about 5000 fungi of Basidiomycetes which may form symbiotic associations. Ascomycetes are also involved in forming ectomycorrhizae on about 2000 plants (Dubey *et al.,* 1999). Ectomycorrhizal fungi act as highly efficient extensions of the host root systems to explore the large area of soil for nutrients and water absorption and translocate them to the host. The host in turn, provides simple carbohydrate as energy source to fungi in the form of photosynthetates. Outside the root surface, fungal mycelia form a compact and multilayered covering known as mantle or fungal sheath. The fungus also forms an intercellular mycelial network in cortex which is known as Hartig net. The mycelia never enter the endodermis.

Fungi forming ectomycorrhizae are *Suillus* spp, *Boletus edulis, Russula* spp, *Scleroderma citrinum, S. aurantium, Cenococcum graniforme, Amanita muscaria, Cenococcus geophilus, Inocybe rimosa, Laccaria laccata, Leccinum, Lepiota, Pisolithus tinctorius, Rhizopogon* spp. etc.

Ectendomycorrhiza: This type of association is found in both gymnosperms and angiosperms. When ectomycorrhizal plant grown in cultivated habitat (Horticultural, Silvicultural etc.) from its natural habitat, they may develop ectendomycorrhizae. Very little research has been done about the fungi involved in this association. This type of mycorrhiza has both the characters of ecto-and endomycorrhiza. The mantle is present but not well developed. The hyphae also penetrate the host cells. Mostly basidiomycetes or ascomycetes form this type of association.

Vesicular Arbuscular Mycorrhizae (VAM) or Arbuscular mycorrhiza (AM): The mycosymbionts are widespread among both cultivated and wild plants. These are found in bryophytes, pteridophytes, gymnosperms and angiosperms (Harley and Smith, 1983). About 90% of vascular plants form this kind of symbiotic association. The fungi forming AM belong to class phycomycetes and family endogonaceae of zygomycotina. Hyphae penetrate both inter as well as intracelluarly. Inside the host root, the hyphae form densely branched arbuscles which also form a tree like haustoria and a sac-like vesicle within the cells. Perhaps, these structures are involved in interchange of food materials between plant and fungus. Fungi forming AM belong to different genera viz., *Endogone, Acaulospora, Gigaspora, Glomus, Enterophosphora, Sclerosystis* and *Scutellospora.*

Ericoid mycorrhiza:

This type of mycorrhiza occur on fine hair root system in the family Ericaceae. Ericoid mycorrhiza are usually associated with woody shrubs. This type of mycorrhiza do not extend beyond host root. The fungi forming ericoid mycorrhiza belong to *Pezizella, Clavaria* spp etc. Many plant genera such as *Epachris, Leucopogon, Monotoa, Rhododendron, Vaccinum* etc. develop ericoid mycorrhiza (Dubey *et al.,* 1999).

Arbutoid mycorrhiza:

Most woody shrubs and trees form arbutoid mycorrhiza. Inside host root there is well defined fungal sheath and Hartig net. The hyphae penetrates the cortical cells. The fungal symbiont in this arbutoid mycorrhiza belong to basidiomycetes. The term ectendomycorrhiza is also applied to the arbutoid mycorrhizae.

Monotropoid mycorrhiza:

The family Monotropaceae develops

monotropoid mycorrhiza. The host root forms a ball like structure which encloses fungal mycelium. This root ball is the surviving organ of Monotropa during unfavorable condition. After the return of favourable conditions, along with the root growth, the fungal sheath and Hartig net develops. Inside epidermal and cortical cells, haustoria like hyphae emerges into the cells. The structure and function of monotropoid mycorrhiza change with seasonal development of the host plants. (Harley and Smith, 1983). The host plant depend on mycorrhizal fungi for organic carbon, although the mechanism of transfer still needs to be investigated.

Orchid mycorrhiza:

The seeds of orchids germinate only when infected with endomycorrhizal fungi. In this type of associations *Rhizoctonia* like mycobionts are involved. There is increasing evidence that some orchids are dependent on fungi that are mycorrhizal with autotrophic plant obtaining organic C from them, as well mineral nutrients derived from the soil. (Smith and Read, 1997).

Ectomycorrhizae: their influence on host.

Ectomycorrhizal basidiomycetes constitute an important element of forest fungal communities (Villeneuve *et al.*, 1989 and Voght *et al.*, 1991) and their unique characteristics as symbionts make them an interesting subject for study on population ecology. Their mycelia maintain a close physiological link to host-tree feeder roots (Read, 1992). Conidia are absent among most species (Hutchinsons, 1989) with only few forming chlamydospores (Agerer, 1991). These fungi therefore rely upon basidiospores, mycelial fragmentation and occasionally sclerotia (Molina *et al.*, 1992), as their principle means of dispersal and reproduction. These fungi have been demonstrated to possess substantial intraspecific variability for a number of traits, including the morphology of ectomycorrhizal roots (Gardes *et al.*, 1990). The ectomycorrhizal roots are characterized by presence of structural components such as fungal sheath or mantle that encloses root, a network of mycelia between epidermis and cortex called Hartig net. Ectomycorrhizae, in addition to its symbiotic functions, mycelium also furnishes inoculum to available root system (Flemming, 1983) and potentially establishes interplant connections (Read, 1992).

Ectomycorrhizae include a great diversity of association. An estimated 2000 fungi can form mycorrhizae with Douglas fir alone (Trappe, 1977) and similar number can be postulated for other host genera, such as pines, oaks and beeches. The majority of ectomycorrhizal fungi are ascomycetes and basidiomycetes that fruit as mushrooms, truffles or cup fungi (Trappe, 1962) only few are zygomycetes.

The ectomycorrhizal fungi show various degree of host specificity. Many can form mycorrhizae with nearly any ectomycorrhizal host (Molina and Trappe, 1982a). Others are specific to a particular host, such as pines or even a sub-group within that genus. Some host shows more selectivity towards mycorrhizal fungi than others. Genera in the Pinaceae will form mycorrhizae with many wide ranging as well as host specific fungi (Molina and Trappe, 1982b).

Pinus kesiya (Royle ex Gordon) an indigenous timber yielding species is dominant at higher altitude of North-Eastern Himalayas in natural forest ecosystem. The roots of pine form a symbiotic mycorrhiza associations with fungi in natural conditions. The *Pinus kesiya* harbors ecto or ectendo mycorrhizal (Sharma, 1981b; Kumar, 1990 and Jha *et al.*, 1990) which helps in establishment, survival and growth of pine seedlings. The selection of suitable ectomycorrhiza fungi for seedlings inoculation can enhance the success of afforestation programmes (Harley and smith, 1983). Many tree species including conifers are able to grow in poor soil condition due to their extensive mycorrhizal root system (Koide and Lu, 1995)

Influence of ectomycorrhizae on nutrient uptake of plants:

Ectomycorrhizal association is specially adapted to nutrient stress condition. Their beneficial role in absorption of inorganic nutrients specially phosphate ions, production and supply of growth regulators, decreasing soil toxicity, increasing resistance to root pathogens and extreme soil temperature is known (Heinrich *et al.* 1989). In absence of ectomycorrhizae, the tree become stunted and yellow or they may even die (Sharma, 1981b). Ectomycorrhizal fungi modify morphology of roots and this change is correlated with the production of cytokinin and other growth hormones, which increase the physiological process of the roots. Non-mycorrhizal seedlings however, fail to survive on nutrient poor soils under natural planting sites, especially during the period of environmental stress (Anderson and Rygiewiez, 1991).

The fungi play a vital role in nutrient cycling, productivity and plant succession and regenerating of the ecosystem. Climatic factors may effect the growth and development of ectomycorrhizal fungi. The studies carried out in laboratory conditions on ectomycorrhizal fungi may, however, show some deficiencies in response to the natural environmental conditions due to complexity in interaction between soil and biological components. It has been found that tree seedlings lacking ectomycorrhizae show severe nutrient deficiencies until mycorrhizae are formed (Trappe and Strand, 1969). Mycorrhizal inoculation improves plant productivity especially in soil with low nutrient status. Artificial inoculation of host plants with specific mycorrhizal fungus may depend upon the efficiency of mycobiont to improve the growth of host under varied ecological conditions (Browning and Whitney, 1993).

Ectomycorrhizae are structurally modified rootlets surrounded by mycobionts and they functions as nutrient absorbing organs. The extrametrical phase extends and function as link between the root system and the soil.

Ectomycorrhizae and nutrient uptake in heavy metal polluted soil:

The use of heavy metals has been increased in various forestry practices in the form of fungicides, pesticides and application of municipal and industrial discharges. The extensive use of domestic sewage in agricultural and forest areas can contribute the toxic heavy metals in soil surface and in ground water.

Toxic metals are numerous and vary in their

action (Gadd, 1993). Microbes may absorb some of these heavy metals and detoxify their effect in soil and rhizosphere region. There are evidences that ectomycorrhizal fungi can evolve metal tolerance.

However, high concentration of heavy metals can cause toxicity in seedlings leading to their stunted growth or in extreme situations the mortality of the seedlings. To evaluate the tolerance range of ectomycorrhizal seedlings of pine (a native tree species of Khasi hills of Meghalaya state) to heavy metals, an experiment was designed using different levels of different heavy metals. The experiment was carried out under glass house conditions. The mycorrhizal fungi used in this experiment were also native and well adapted to the local environmental conditions. The mycorrhizal fungi induced resistance against heavy metal pollution but at higher levels, these could not sustain it with the same efficiency as was done at low concentrations of the pollutants. The efficiency of mycorrhizae in uptake of N, P and K may be reduced up to 50% and up to 70% in non-mycorrhizal seedlings at higher levels of heavy metals present in the soil. However, long term effect of heavy metal pollutants on mycorrhizal and non-mycorrhizal seedlings, the dilution of pollutants by mycorrhizae and other associative microbes need to be studied. Studies on nutrient content of seedlings applied with different concentration of heavy metals has shown that the content of nutrient as a whole were adversely affected by the presence of heavy metals. (Tables 2.2-2.4).

Table 2.2: Effect of heavy metals on nitrogen content (%) in mycorrhizal and non- mycorrhizal seedlings.

Metals conc. (ppm)	Non-mycorrhizal seedlings (Control)	Nitrogen content (%) in mycorrhizal seedlings			
		M1	M2	M3	M4
0	0.99	2.00	2.00	2.00	2.00
Zn10	0.91	1.87	2.25	1.93	1.83
Zn50	0.80	1.80	2.19	1.86	1.72
Zn100	0.69	1.57	1.92	1.79	1.56
Zn200	0.66	1.54	1.75	1.72	1.51
Zn500	0.64	1.52	1.61	1.61	1.05
Ni10	0.97	1.72	1.88	1.90	1.87
Ni50	0.91	1.64	1.79	1.77	1.76
Ni100	0.78	1.52	1.72	1.72	1.66
Ni200	0.72	1.42	1.58	1.70	1.63
Ni500	0.70	1.41	1.47	1.61	1.52
Al10	0.98	1.65	2.03	1.95	2.04
Al50	0.92	1.62	1.91	1.91	1.94
Al100	0.85	1.59	1.65	1.75	1.91
Al200	0.80	1.48	1.56	1.72	1.80
Al500	0.79	1.47	1.35	1.66	1.78
Cd10	0.95	1.71	2.11	2.01	2.12
Cd50	0.92	1.68	1.92	1.90	1.90
Cd100	0.86	1.62	1.90	1.89	1.70
Cd200	0.85	1.58	1.80	1.83	1.70
Cd500	0.80	1.42	1.75	1.61	1.53
Cu10	1.01	1.53	1.92	2.09	2.11
Cu50	0.91	1.50	1.68	1.89	1.87
Cu100	0.81	1.48	1.60	1.69	1.80
Cu200	0.66	1.46	1.58	1.64	1.57
Cu500	0.63	1.34	1.55	1.59	1.50
Pb10	0.96	1.90	1.62	1.81	1.90
Pb50	0.85	1.75	1.67	1.70	1.90
Pb100	0.73	1.63	1.60	1.63	1.88
Pb200	0.68	1.38	1.58	1.44	1.81

Pb500	0.63	1.34	1.51	1.40	1.52

M1=*Scleroderma aurantium*, M2= *Boletus* sp, M3= *Cenococcum graniforme*, M4= *Suillus luteus*.

Table 2.3: Effect of heavy metals on potassium content (%) in mycorrhizal and non-Mycorrhizal seedlings

Metals conc. (ppm)	Non-mycorrhizal seedlings (Control)	Nitrogen content (%) in mycorrhizal seedlings			
		M1	M2	M3	M4
0	0.80	0.90	0.90	0.90	0.90
Zn10	0.70	0.78	0.84	0.89	0.84
Zn50	0.70	0.78	0.84	0.89	0.84
Zn100	0.60	0.68	0.78	0.72	0.78
Zn200	0.41	0.60	0.59	0.64	0.61
Zn500	0.33	0.52	0.57	0.58	0.45
Ni10	0.69	0.75	1.00	0.73	0.81
Ni50	0.47	0.70	0.84	0.56	0.59
Ni100	0.36	0.67	0.65	0.53	0.50
Ni200	0.31	0.58	0.61	0.40	0.42
Ni500	0.25	0.53	0.50	0.35	0.30
Ai10	0.71	0.75	0.78	0.86	0.97
Al50	0.63	0.68	0.69	0.75	0.77
Al100	0.51	0.62	0.58	0.60	0.69
Al200	0.50	0.60	0.55	0.52	0.57
Al500	0.33	0.52	0.46	0.40	0.47
Cd10	0.75	0.76	0.82	0.97	0.68
Cd50	0.60	0.63	0.78	0.87	0.65
Cd100	0.49	0.56	0.67	0.65	0.65
Cd200	0.40	0.47	0.44	0.43	0.47
Cd500	0.41	0.45	0.47	0.56	0.45
Cu10	0.62	0.69	0.70	0.72	0.83
Cu50	0.40	0.65	0.64	0.68	0.76

Cu100	0.34	0.58	0.52	0.59	0.70
Cu200	0.30	0.50	0.48	0.51	0.52
Cu500	0.40	0.47	0.44	0.43	0.47
Pb10	0.58	0.58	0.68	0.82	0.72
Pb50	0.56	0.62	0.62	0.78	0.61
Pb100	0.51	0.55	0.57	0.71	0.54
Pb200	0.44	0.51	0.53	0.68	0.53
Pb500	0.40	0.47	0.50	0.61	0.51

M1= *Scleroderma aurantium*, M2= *Boletus* sp, M3= *Cenococcum graniforme*, M4= *Suillus luteus*.

Table 2.4: Effect of heavy metals on phosphorus content (%) in mycorrhizal and non-Mycorrhizal seedlings

Metals conc. (ppm)	Non-mycorrhizal seedlings (Control)	Nitrogen content (%) in mycorrhizal seedlings			
		M1	M2	M3	M4
0	0.78	0.88	0.88	0.88	0.88
Zn10	0.65	0.81	0.90	0.89	0.86
Zn50	0.59	0.86	0.82	0.82	0.70
Zn100	0.51	0.78	0.66	0.78	0.69
Zn200	0.39	0.66	0.0.63	0.62	0.45
Zn500	0.35	0.61	0.61	0.60	0.42
Ni10	0.67	0.86	0.70	0.87	0.89
Ni50	0.60	0.80	0.66	0.70	0.80
Ni100	0.55	0.79	0.61	0.65	0.67
Ni200	0.51	0.62	0.59	0.63	0.65
Ni500	0.48	0.56	0.50	0.56	0.59
Al10	0.69	0.73	0.68	0.88	0.79
Al50	0.61	0.68	0.63	0.71	0.74
Al100	0.49	0.55	0.55	0.62	0.72
Al200	0.49	0.53	0.50	0.63	0.59
Al500	0.48	0.51	0.49	0.55	0.55

Cd10	0.69	0.90	0.74	0.79	0.90
Cd50	0.61	0.89	0.66	0.69	0.80
Cd100	0.60	0.76	0.63	0.61	0.74
Cd200	0.51	0.59	0.55	0.55	0.66
Cd500	0.49	0.53	0.53	0.51	0.55
Cu10	0.73	0.89	0.83	0.87	0.84
Cu50	0.60	0.80	0.82	0.80	0.73
Cu100	0.58	0.70	0.72	0.69	0.69
Cu200	0.55	0.61	0.68	0.65	0.60
Cu500	0.50	0.60	0.59	0.55	0.54
Pb10	0.74	0.81	0.86	0.88	0.90
Pb50	0.61	0.72	0.80	0.86	0.84
Pb100	0.60	0.67	0.70	0.76	0.70
Pb200	0.51	0.60	0.63	0.73	0.65
Pb500	0.44	0.53	0.50	0.59	0.55

M1= *Scleroderma aurantium*, M2= *Boletus* sp, M3= *Cenococcum graniforme*, M4= *Suillus luteus*.

Table 2.5: Effect of heavy metals on nitrogen, phosphorus and potassium contents in mycorrhizal and non-mycorrhizal seedlings treated with mixed mycobionts.

Metals	Nitrogen (%)		Phosphorus (%)		Potassium (%)	
conc. (ppm)	MMF	Control	MMF	Control	MMF	Control
0	2.50	1.91	1.21	0.90	1.23	0.93
Zn10	2.31	1.91	0.96	0.79	1.14	0.88
Zn50	2.25	1.82	0.84	0.70	1.03	0.87
Zn100	2.20	1.74	0.80	0.62	0.97	0.76
Zn200	1.78	1.32	0.70	0.65	0.91	0.65
Zn500	1.62	1.09	0.67	0.50	0.80	0.59
Ni10	2.49	1.28	0.91	0.80	1.02	0.92
Ni50	1.98	1.21	0.80	0.69	0.96	0.90
Ni100	1.91	1.16	0.71	0.60	0.92	0.83
Ni200	1.84	1.08	0.69	0.51	0.87	0.80
Ni500	1.69	1.00	.056	0.40	0.73	0.60

Al10	2.48	1.85	0.89	0.71	0.95	0.89
Al50	2.40	1.80	0.81	0.67	0.90	0.83
Al100	2.33	1.75	0.78	0.59	0.89	0.73
Al200	1.92	1.58	0.63	0.56	0.71	0.63
Al500	1.75	1.32	0.59	0.40	0.69	0.61
Cd10	2.29	1.92	0.93	0.74	1.07	1.00
Cd50	2.21	1.82	0.79	0.70	1.05	0.95
Cd100	1.89	1.10	0.73	0.67	0.83	0.76
Cd200	1.81	1.08	0.70	0.62	0.79	0.75
Cd500	1.68	1.04	0.60	0.42	0.66	0.60
Cu10	2.07	1.16	0.90	0.81	1.04	1.24
Cu50	1.98	1.05	0.86	0.69	1.07	0.85
Cu100	1.70	1.01	0.80	0.70	0.98	0.62
Cu200	1.67	0.97	0.73	0.61	0.93	0.61
Cu500	1.02	0.87	0.62	0.43	0.86	0.57
Pb10	1.61	1.18	0.94	0.85	1.17	1.10
Pb50	1.47	1.18	0.86	0.76	1.11	1.02
Pb100	1.39	1.08	0.80	0.70	0.81	0.78
Pb200	1.34	1.01	0.75	0.50	0.78	0.71
Pb500	1.34	0.99	0.67	0.35	0.73	0.70

MMF= Seedlings inoculated with mixed mycorrhizal fungi

The metal induced damages were seen at 50 ppm and above of the heavy metal treated seedlings. The mixed mycobionts inoculated seedlings exhibited maximum uptake of nitrogen, phosphorus and potassium as compared to that of individual inoculated symbionts (table 2.5). The higher contents of mineral nutrients in seedlings suggested that growth was greater in the mycorrhizal seedlings than non-mycorrhizal ones. This has been related to the increased root surface area (Harley and smith, 1983).

Current evidence obtained with plant exposed to heavy metal indicates that the cause of growth reduction in non-mycorrhizal plants may be mainly due to their nitrogen status. Since nitrogen is the growth limiting factor, any change in nitrogen uptake and transport would alter the growth of plant. Nitrogen content in shoot is directly related to the relative growth rate of plants (Ingestad. *et al.*, 1986), this is in support of our results also.

Study on heavy metals demonstrates that the inoculation of mixed inoculum increased uptake of NPK by mycorrhizal seedlings at different levels of application metals. Mycobionts may be more advantageous to both plant and fungus, which could permit the host to explore more mineral resources effectively. There was clear evidence that Cd and other heavy metals influenced the translocation of essential elements (Smith and Brennan, 1984). Cd, Ni and Pb are considered extremely toxic metals in plants causing disorder in photosynthetic machinery even at relatively low concentration resulting in growth reduction of seedlings (Tinker, 1981)

In the recent findings the greater root development in the seedlings treated with 50 ppm or less of heavy metals might have accounted for higher NPK accumulation. The enhanced heavy metal accumulation in non-mycorrhizal roots may be partially responsible for poor root development (Tan *et al.*, 1990b) which will lead to the less exploitation of mineral nutrients due to their reduced root system.

Mycorrhizal association is specially adapted to nutrient stress condition (Heinrich *et al.*, 1989), it may be possible that under these circumstances, ectomycroohizal roots and their mycelia function as mineral source sink than non-mycorrhizal ones. Reduced growth of the extramycelium resulting from the high concentration of heavy metals is likely to reduce the potential of the fungus to take up minerals and water and transfer them to the seedlings.

Mycorrhizal development might be a more important factor than soil nutrient availability for determining nutrient levels especially for phosphorus due to its low mobility in the soil. Dighton *et al.*, (1990) demonstrated mineral nutrient availability in plants due to reduced absorbing surface of mycorrhizae caused by pollution which has resulted in rapid decline of forest. Similar decrease in nutrient concentration in seedlings has been reported due to Ni toxicity (Cataldo *et al.*, 1978). The main cause of reduced nutrient content of the seedlings was due to the high concentration of Cu, Ni, Cd, Pb, Zn and Al in soil which restricted the development of mycorrhizae in the root system. In the present investigation, the nutrient concentration in the seedlings has shown that the lower levels of heavy metals were able to sustain growth of non-mycorrhizal and mycorrhizal seedlings.

The data processed by analysis of variance (ANOVA) showed a positive correlation between mycorrhizal infection and N, P and K ($p<0.01$ and $p<0.05$) uptake (table 2.6). The data analysis also showed a significant variation between mycorrhizal and non-mycorrhizal seedlings in N ($p<0.01$), K and P ($p<0.05$) uptake (table 2.7).

Table 2.6: Correlation coefficient (r) of mycorrhizal infection (%) with various parameters in pots and field pine seedlings

	Mycorrhizal infection						
Parameters	M1	M2	M3	M4	NM	MMF	NM
Nitrogen	0.89*	0.96*	0.80**	0.92*	NS	0.99*	NS
Phosphorus	0.79**	0.93*	0.88*	0.90*	NS	0.91*	NS
Potassium	0.92*	0.93*	0.96*	0.97*	NS	0.90*	NS

M1=*C. graniforme*, M2= *S. leutus*, M3= *Boletus* sp, M4= *S. aurantium* NM= Non-mycorrhizal, Mmf= Mixed mycorrhizal fungi.

*= significant at p<0.01 level, ** = significant at p<0.05 level.

Table 2.7: Analysis of variance (F) values of various mycobionts, mycorrhizal and non-mycorrhizal and pots and field with various parameters in pine seedlings

Source of Variance	variation between mycobionts	variation between mycorrhizal & non-mycorr-hizal	variation between pots and fields
Nitrogen	NS	2.97*	5.49*
Phosphorus	NS	2.76**	2.52*
Potassium	NS	2.48**	4.27**

•= significant at p< 0.01 level, ** = significant at p<0.05 level.

The main effect of metal treatment in non-mycorrhizal seedlings was directly correlated to the nutrient availability. At high levels of metals, however, inhibition of nutrient contents may be due to complexing ability of the heavy metals. In these circumstances, the presence of an ectomycorrhizal fungal symbiont could be of considerable importance.

Though, studies on myccorrhizae have received enough attention during the past few years, however, their interaction in relation to environmental factors need careful investigation particularly in relation to the soil pollution caused by heavy metals.

References:

Agerer, R. 1991. Ectomycorrhizae of *Sarcodon imbricatus* on Norway spruce and their chlamydospores. Mycorrhizae. 1:20-30.

Anderson, C. P. and Rygwiewiez, P. T. 1991. Stress-response interaction and mycorrhizal plant: Understanding carbon allocation priorities: Environ Pollution. 73: 217-224

Browning, M. H. R. and Whitney, R. D. 1993. Infection of containerized jack pine and black spruce by *Laccaria* species and *Thelephora terrestris* and seedling survival and growth after out planting. Can. J. For. Res. 23:330-333.

Cataldo, D. A. Garland, T. R. and Wildung, R. E. 1978. Nickel in plants 1. uptake kinetics intact soyabean seedlings. Plant Physiol. 62:563-565.

Dighton, J. and Jansen, S. E. 1990. Effect of air pollutants on ectomycorrhizas. Air Pollution Research Report. 30:EEC. Brussels.

Dubey, R. C. and Maheshwari, D. K. 1999. In: Text book of microbiology. Microbial ecology II: Soil Microbiology. 561-582.

Flemming, L. V. 1983. Succession of mycorrhizal fungi on the birch infection of seedlings planted around matured trees. Plant and Soil. 71: 263-267.

Gadd, G.M. 1993. Interaction of fungi with toxic metals. New Phytol. 124:330-333.

Gardes, M., Wong, K. K. Y. and Fortin, J. A. 1990. Interactions between monokaryotic and dikaryotic isolates of *Laccaria bicolor* on roots of *Pinus banksiana*. Symbiosis. 8:233-250.

Harley, J. L. and Smith, S. E. 1983. Mycorrhizal symbiosis. Academic Press London. P-461.

Heinrich, P. A., Mulligan, D. R. and Pattrick, J. W. 1989. The effect of ectomycorrhizae on the phosphorus and dry weight acquisition of Eucalyptus seedlings. Plant and Soil. 109:147-149.

Hutchinsons, L. T. 1989. Absence of conidia as a morphological character in ectomycorrhizal fungi. Mycologia. 81:587-594.

Ingestad, T., Arverby, A. S. and Kahr, M. 1986. The influence of ectomycorrhizae on nitrogen nutrition and growth of *Pinus sylvestries* seedlings. Physiologia Planatarium. 68:575-582.

Jha, B. N., Sharma, G. D. and Mishra, R. R. 1990. Effect of pH on the growth of ectomycorrhizal fungi in vitro. Proc. Natn. Con. Mycorrhizae, Haryana Agric. Univ. Hisar (eds. B. L Jalal and H. Chand). 66-67.

Koide, R. T. and Lu, X. 1995. On the cause of offspring superiority confers by mycorrhizal infection of *Abutilon theoparti*. New Phytol. 131: 435-441.

Kumar, R. 1990. Ecological investigation on ectomycorrhizae of Khasi pine (*Pinus kesiya* Royle ex Gordon) in different soil conditions. Ph. D Thesis, North Eastern Hill Univ. Shillong.

Molina, R. and Trappe, J. 1982a. Lack of mycorrhizal specificity by the ericaceous hosts *Arbustus menzjesu* and *Arctostaphylos uva-ursj*. New Phytol. 90:495-509.

Molina, R. and Trappe, J. 1982b. Patterns of ectomycorrhizal host specificity and potential among Pacific North-West conifers and fungi. For. Sci. 28:243-258.

Molina, R., Massicotte, H. and Trappe, J. 1992. Specificity phenomena in mycorrhizal symbiosis community ecological consequences and practical implications. In mycorrhizal functioning an integrative plant-fungal process. Edited by M. F. Allen. Routlege. Chapman and Hall. Inc. New York. 357-423.

Read, D. J. 1991. Mycorrhizas in ecosystems. Experientia. 47:376-391.

Read, D. J. 1992. The mycorrhizae in mycelium. In: Allen; MF (Ed.)

Mycorrhizal functioning: an integrative plant-fungal process. Routlege, Chapman and Hall, New York. 102-133.

Sharma, G. D. 1981b. Influence of mycorrhizal developmental stages and plant age on rhizosphere population on *Pinus kesiya*. Acta. Mycologia (Poland) 17: 45-51.

Smith, G. C. and Brennan, E. 1984. response of silver maple seedlings to an acute dose of root applied with cadmium. For. Sci. 30:582-586.

Smith, S. E. and Read, D. J. 1997. Mycorrhizal Symbiosis. 2nd Ed. London. Academic Press Ltd.

Tan, H. and Keltjens, W. G. 1990b. Interaction between Al and phosphorus plants. I. Studies with Al-sensitive sorghum genotype. TAM. 428. Plants and Soil. 124:15-23.

Tinker, P. B. 1981. Levels, distribution and chemical forms of trace elements in food plants. Physiological Transactions of Royal Society London. 294: 41-55.

Trappe, J. M. 1962. *Cenococcum graniforme* in its distribution, ecology, mycorrhizal formation, inherent variation. Ph. D. Thesis. Univ. Wash. Seattle. 148.

Trappe, J. M. and Strand, R. F. 1969. Mycorrhizal deficiency in a Douglas-fir region nursery. Forest Science. 15: 381-389.

Trappe, J. M. 1977. Selection of fungi for mycorrhizal inoculation in nurseries. Annual Review of Phytophatology. 15: 203-222.

Villeneuve, N., Grantner, N. M. and Fortin, J. A. 1989. Freguency and diversity of ectomycorrhizal and saprophytic fungi in the Laurentide mountain of Quebic. Can. J. Bot. 67: 2616-2629.

Vogt, K. A., Publicover, D. A. and Vogt, D. J. 1991. A critique of the role of mycorrhizae in forest ecology. Agric. Ecosys. Environ. 35:171-190.

Heavy Metal Pollution and Mycorrhiza : **43-55**
Authors : Prof. G. D. Sharma and Dr. Tali Ajungla
Today & Tomorrow's Printers and Publishers. New Delhi-110 002

Chapter 3

Heavy metals on the formation of ectomycorrhizae:

Morphological characteristics:

Modified Melin Norkhran's medium (MMN) was used for culture of ectomycorrhizal fungi. Four ectomycorrhizal fungi were isolated and tested for the synthesis of mycorrhizal association. *Cenoccocum graniforme* was isolated from sclerotia while *Boletus* sp., *Scleroderma aurantium* and *Suillus luteus* were isolated from sporocarps (table 3.1).

Table 3.1: Source, place of collection and host of the ectomycorrhizal fungi

Ectomycorrhi-Zal fungi	Source of isolation	place of collection	Host
Cenoccocum graniforme	sclerotia	NEHU campus pine forest, Shillong	*Pinus kesiya*
Scleroderma aurantium	sporocarps	NEHU campus pine forest, Shillong	*Pinus kesiya*
Boletus sp	sporocarps	NEHU campus pine forest, Shillong	*Pinus kesiya*
Suillus luteus	sporocarps	NEHU campus pine forest, Shillong	*Pinus kesiya*

The morphological characters of sporocarps (fig. A, B & C) and radial growth were used for identification of fungi using the keys outlined by Singer (1962, 1975). The characteristics features of fungi on MMN media are described here.

Cenoccocum graniforme: Fungal colony black and rough in texture, round with regular margin; aerial hyphae absent and the growth of fungus slow. Wet colony on the upper surface, mycelia black in colour, compactly interwoven, formed sclerotia under dried condition. Hyphal size 8.3 µm: with digitate rough in texture. Mycorrhiza dichotomously bifurcated or singly thickened at the tip of tertiary root and black with external hyphae.

Scleroderma aurantium: Peridium thick, split into polygonal scales, coarse in texture, sub-globose, gleba blackish, strong odour, spores brown, carpophore diameter 7-10 cm, spiny, 4-9 µm. Fungal colony grey, rough in texture, mycelia closely interwoven, aerial hyphae absent. Warty appearance with irregular margin. Hyphal size 7.5 µm. Mycorrhizae dichotomously branched. And white to yellow with smooth texture.

Boletus sp. Sporophore 5.-10 cm high, cap 5-7 cm, convex, smooth, viscous in damp weather, pale yellow in young stage and light brown towards maturity. Pore small, circular, stipe smooth, pleasant odour, spore olive brown, fusiform 4-6 µm. fungal colony light brown, aerial hyphae present, mycelium closely interwoven, hyphal size 9.1 µm. Mycorrhizae coralloid and creamy with small texture.

Suillus luteus: Sporophore 4-8 cm high, cap size 4-6 cm, convex, presenting conical appereance, margin regular, cuticle viscous in damp weather, grayish brown, pore tiny polygonal. Fungal colony, light brown with aerial hyphae. Mycelium closely interwoven. Hyphal size 9.4 µm. Mycorrhizae white and dichotomously branched with smooth texture.

The mating type and mycelial growth rate are summarized in table 3.2 indicating the relative size of colonies, sector formation, zones of migration of hyphal development.

Table 3.2: Morphological characteristics of mycorrhizae formed by different ectomycorrhizal fungi.

Ectomycorr-hizal fungi	Morphology of of mycorrhizae	Colour of mycorrhizae	Texture of mycorrhizae
Cenococcum graniforme	Digitate type	Black	Rough
Scleroderma aurantium	Dichotomously branched	White to yellowish	Smooth
Boletus sp	Coralloid type	Creamy	Smooth
Suillus luteus	Dichotomously branched	Yellowish white	Smooth

Structural characteristics of ectomycorrhizae in heavy metal exposed soil:

Morphological characteristics of mycorrhizae have been shown in fig. D, E, F &G.

Observation of ectomycorrhizae and non-mycorrhizal short roots by electron microscopy showed variation in the cells due to high concentration of metals. Cytological characteristics of the mycorrhizal fungi altered with increased concentration of heavy metals such as Cd, Pb, Cu. Ni, Zn and Al. The fungal cytoplasm appeared more disrupted at higher concentration of the heavy metals. The hyphae penetrated root directly, with comparatively fewer infection points between the anticlinal walls of epidermal cells or through the root hairs across their distal or basal part. Dense fungal structures are formed mainly in the inner layer forming branches penetrating into deeper cortex (fig. H). White fungal patches, interwoven strands were formed extending out from mycorrhizal mantle. (fig. I). Several fruiting bodies were formed and hyphal strands were clearly visible. *Scleroderma aurantium* colonized the root within 6-7 weeks and formed extensive extrametrical mycelium (fig. J) and thick mycelial strands were developed in all root chamber but were lacking in seedlings with higher concentration of metals. *Boletus* sp was also a rapid colonizer. *Suillus luteus* and *Cenococcum graniforme* colonized the root intensively after 4-6 weeks. The growth of these species was visible from the early stage of seedlings growth. After intensive colonization of the root the growth of mycelium slowed down particularly of *C. graniforme*. However, small strands were formed during last period specially on the plants treated with 10 ppm and 50 ppm of heavy metals.

Effect of heavy metals on mycorrhizal system:

Cd and Ni toxicity symptoms on the mycorrhizal fungi showed diverse effect. Some species seemed to be extremely sensitive, whereas others remained unaffected, as measured by the presence of the living extrametrical mycelium at the end (fig. L). Although, these fungi were seriously damaged by addition of high concentration of heavy metals, however, the mycorrhizal association did not disappear completely from the root system (fig. M). the density of mycelium greatly reduced in heavy metals treated plants compared to control mycorrhizal plants. Dead mycorrhizal mycelium were often colonized by saprophytic microorganisms, which may increase the values of fungal biomass.

The effect of Cu, Ni and Pb on the mycorrhizal fungi were variable. In some plants mycelium was able to persist and to recover somewhat whereas in others the mycelium did not ameliorate (fig. N). In case of Al treated seedlings visual symptoms of Al toxicity in non-mycorrhiza such as thickened and dark root tips were seen at all concentrations of 50 ppm and above of heavy metals. In ectomycorrhizal roots these symptoms occurred only in small part of the root system. Although, mycorrhizal infection was observed at all level of concentrations of heavy metals in the mycorrhizal roots, short root bifurcations were less at 100 ppm and above, which resulted in less penetration of fungi inside the cortical cells.. the ectomycorrhizal and non-mycorrhizal roots exposed to high dose of heavy metals had all distorted cytoplasm (fig.O).

In mycorrhizal roots, the fungal sheath function as a barrier for toxic metals. In this way mycorrhizae can help higher plants to adapt and to survive in contaminated habitats (Wilkinson and Dickinson, 1995).

The results demonstrate that the presence of Pb 50 ppm and above also significantly reduced mycorrhizal infection. Higher level of Cd and Ni checked the mycorrhizal formation on seedlings root system and significantly decreased mycorrhizal infection. Stunted seedlings which resulted due to high concentration of heavy metals had several thick electron dense cells. The fungal cells had thin walls and there were no Hartig net formation. This was in marked contrast with controlled seedlings where no heavy metals were added. The electron dense cells were widely scattered and fungal hyphae readily entered the cortex of the host to form well developed Hartig net (fig. P). these morphological and cytological effects may be due to the toxic nature of heavy metals.

Higher concentration of dissolved Al has resulted in the screening of many forest tree species especially for Al sensitivity (Anderson 1988., Shaedle *et a.l*, 1989). Mycorrhizal fungi may effect the response of trees to Al (Harley and Smith, 1983). In Al-stressed plants, recently, there has been an ardent discussion about what comes first: inhibition of root cell elongation or inhibition of root cell division. In Al-stressed *Zea mays*, Al-induced alterations in root cap cells have been observed before root elongation was inhibited (Johnson and Bennet, 1991).

Recent investigation reveal that all the heavy metals induced cellular changes in the symbiont which appeared as a faint appearance of plasma membrane, increasing transparency and gradual granulation of cytoplasm and swelling of mitochondria and cristae. These changes were first observed in the mantle. The mantle varied from 23 to 26μm in thickness and the hyphae of the Hartig net frequently penetrated all cortical cells up to endodermis in ectomycorrhizal roots which were treated with lower concentration of heavy metals. In case of seedlings treated with 100 ppm, 200 ppm and 500 ppm of heavy metals, the fungal mantle thickness ranging from 11 to 18µm in thickness and the hyphae of the Hartig net rarely penetrated deeper between the first layer of cortical cells.

Results have clearly indicated that the application of heavy metals to soil was toxic to the development of mycorrhizae with *Pinus kesiya* seedlings. Reduction of ectomycorrhizal development may be due to the effect of high concentration of metals on synthesis of protein/nucleic acids in cells of mycobiont and effectiveness of Cd, Ni, Zn, Pb, Cu and Al which became toxic to the external mycelium. Root exudates are important factors in governing mycorrhizal colonization (Duchesne *et al.,* 1989). Perhaps heavy metals altered the root exudation in a way which did not favor the multiplication of mycorrhizal fungi (Schwab *et al.,* 1982). The importance of ectomycorrhizal fungi and their ability to grow in presence of heavy metals though to a lesser extent could be due to their colonization and ability to detoxify them. Deacon and Flemming (1992) considered that short roots are the primary resource unit for mycorrhizal interaction and the root colonization to be determined mainly by competitive exclusion because of superior colonization, with mycelial inoculum potential, growth rate, host specificity and abiotic factors influencing mycobiont success.

It has been observed that concentration of heavy metals limited the mycelium production and its colonization into deeper cortex. The cytological interactions in the fungal hyphae with increase in heavy metals concentration also suggested an accumulation of heavy metals in the fungal mantle. However, these also may have occurred if mycorrhizal fungus were more sensitive to these metals than the host. The cellular and structural changes in host root could be due to breakdown of cytoplasmic structure, disruption of cell walls and cortical cells and accumulation of the dense compound. The cytological changes observed in metal-stressed pine root were similar to those that occurred in seedlings in which nutrient deficiency was induced deliberately (Fink, 1991). It has been shown that in *Agrostis tenuis* the metal is confined to the roots, the main site of complexing being cell wall (Wu *et al.*, 1975). At high levels of metals. However, inhibition of root extension and hence complexing ability occurred. In these circumstances, presence of an ectomycorrhizal fungal symbiont could be of considerable importance.

Fungal cell walls known to have strong affinities for metallic cations (Ashida *et al.*, 1975) which provide greater concentration of fungal material in the root, particularly efficient exclusion mechanism. Elaborate hyphal coils occupy most of the cortical cells of the host root, with lower concentration of metals to which absorption occurs these would provide a greatly increased surface for retention of metals ions.

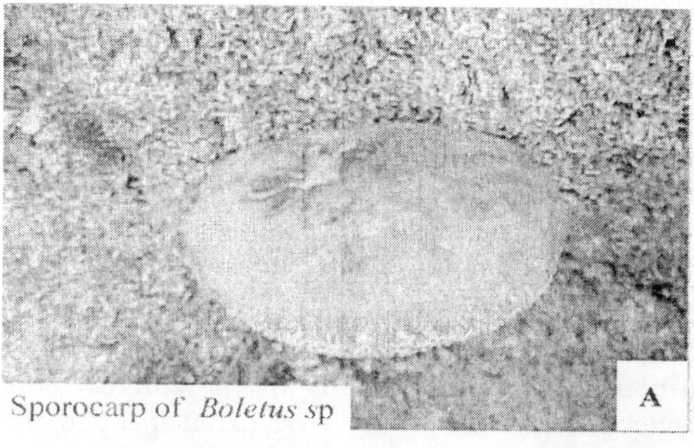

Fig A: Sporocarp of *Boletus* sp in mixed forest condition

Fig B: Sporocarp of *S. aurantium* under pine dominated forest

Fig C: Sporocarp of *S. luteus* under natural condition

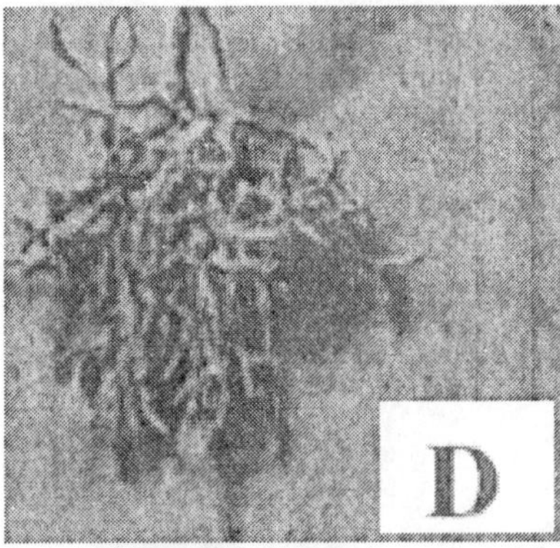

Fig D:*Pinus* roots infected with *Scleroderma* sp

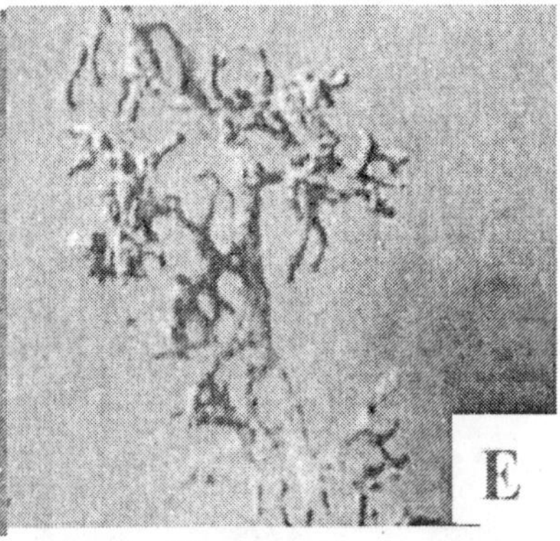

Fig E: *Pinus* roots infected with *Boletus* sp

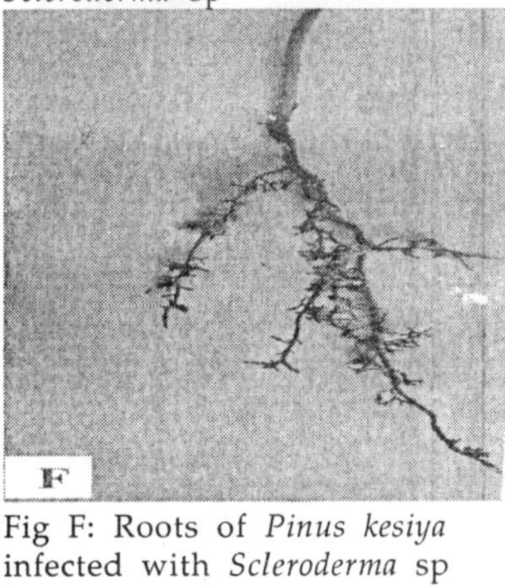

Fig F: Roots of *Pinus kesiya* infected with *Scleroderma* sp

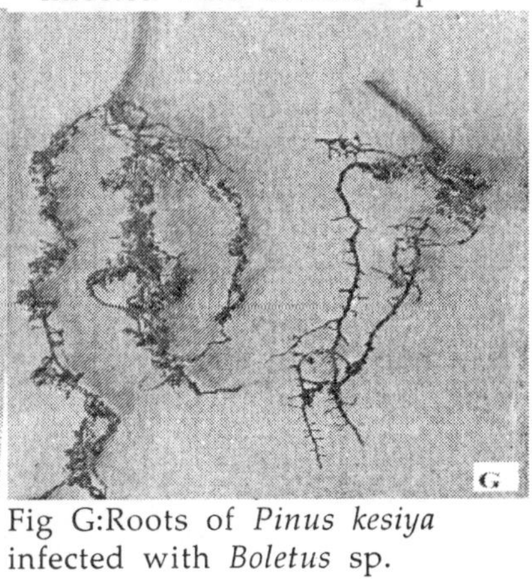

Fig G:Roots of *Pinus kesiya* infected with *Boletus* sp.

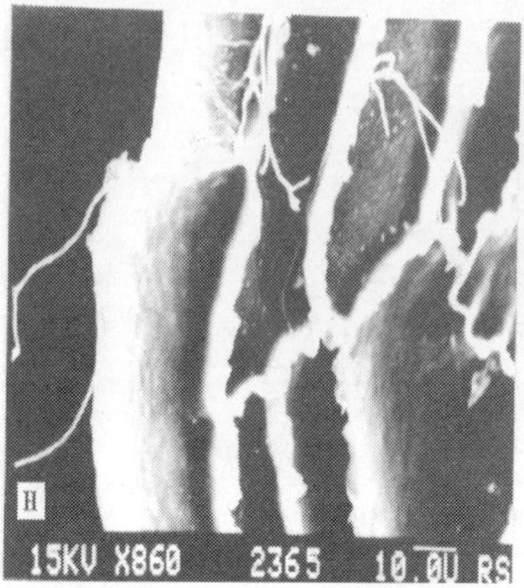

Fig H: Infected with *Suillus luteus* and treated with Zn 10 ppm, showing

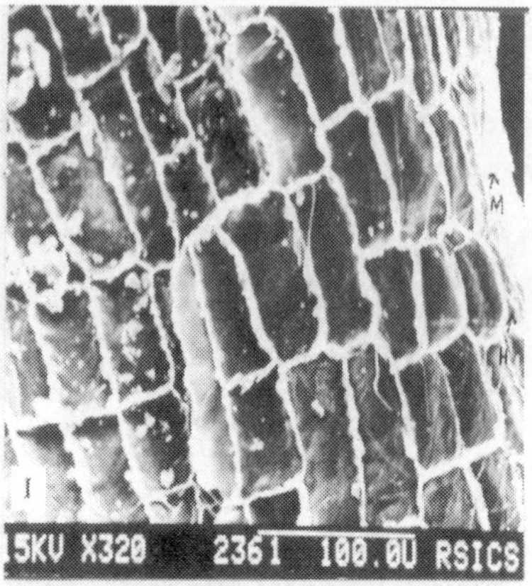

Fig I: Infected with Boletus sp and treated with Cd 10ppm, showing mantle and Hartig net.

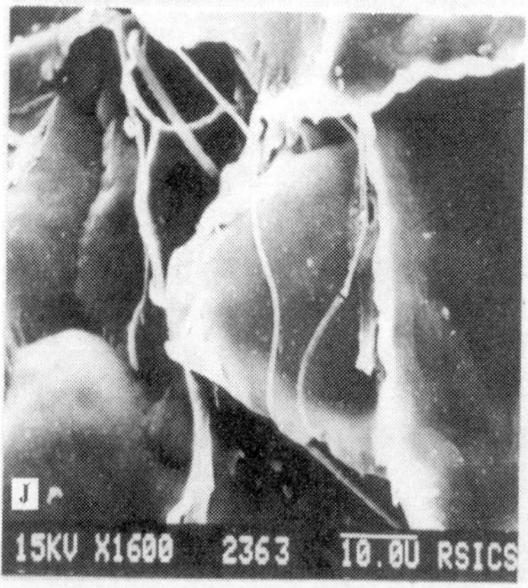

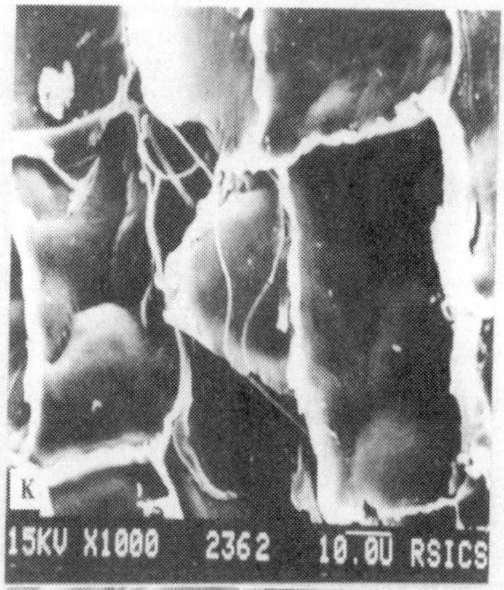

Fig J and K: infected with *Scleroderma aurantium* and treated with Cu 10ppm showing extrametrical mycelia

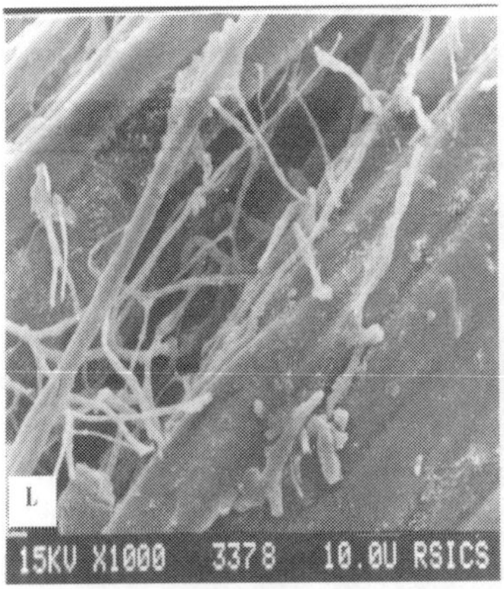

Fig L: Infected with *Suillus luteus* and treated with Ni10ppm, showing mycelium

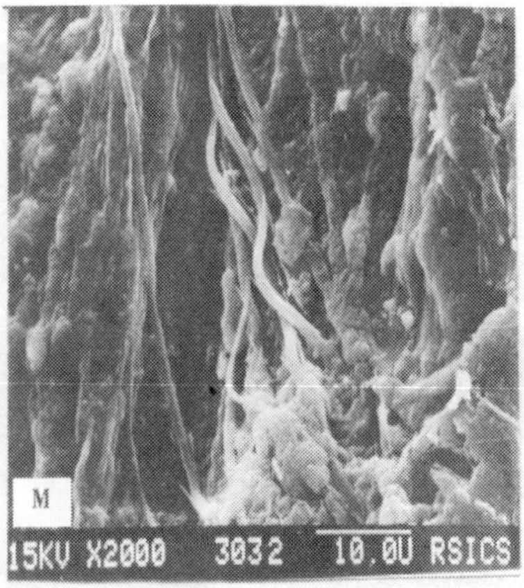

Fig M: Infected with *Boletus* sp treated with Al 500ppm showing damaged due to Al toxicity

Fig N: Infected with *Cenococcum graniforme* and treated with Ni 500ppm showing distorted cytoplasm

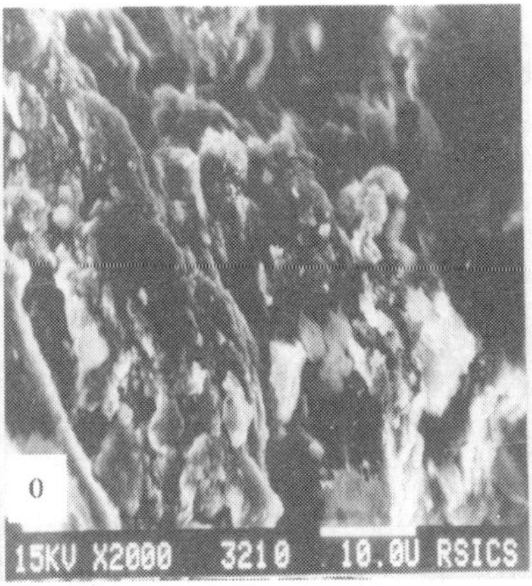

Fig O: Non-mycorrhizal root exposed to Pb 500ppm, showing damaged by Pb toxicity.

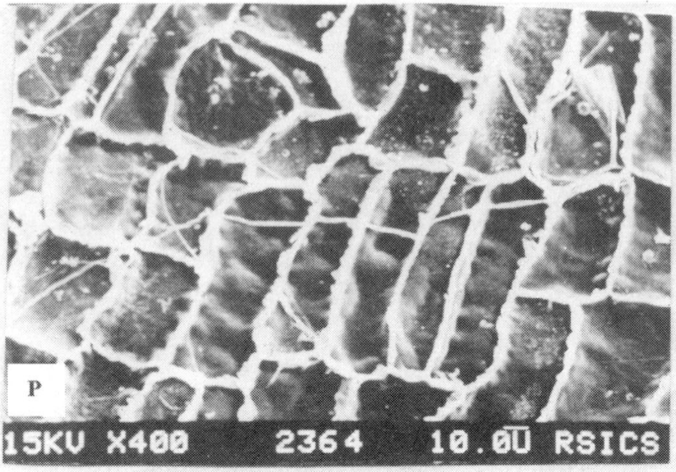

Fig P: Ectomycorrhizal roots showing well developed Hartig net and mantle.

References:

Anderson, M. 1988. Toxicity and tolerance of aluminium in vascular plants. Water Air Soil Pollution. 39:439-462.

Ashida, J., Higashi, N. and Kikuchi, T. 1975. Protoplasma. 57: 27-32.

Duschene, L. C., Peterson, R. L. and Ellis, B. E. 1989. The time course of disease suppression and antibiosis by the ectomycorrhizal fungus *Paxillus involutus*. New Phytol. 112: 693-698.

Fink, S. 1991. Structural changes in coniferous needles due to Mg and K deficiency. Fert. Res. 27:23-27.

Harley, J. L. and Smith, S. E. 1983. Mycorrhizal Symbiosis. Academic Press. London.

Johnson, P. A. and Bennet, R. J. 1991. Aluminium tolerance of root cap cells. J. Plant Physiol. 137:760-762.

Schwab, S. M., Johnson, E. L. V. and Menge, J. A. 1982. Influence of Simazine on formation of vesicular-arbuscular mycorrhizae in *Chempodium quinona* Willd. Plant Soil. 64:283-287.

Shaedle, M., Thorton, F. C., Raynal, D. J. and Tepper, H. B. 1989. Response of tree seedlings to aluminium. Tree Physiol. 5:337-356.

Singer, R. 1962. The agaricales in modern taxonomy. Gramer, Wienhein. 915.

Singer, R. 1975. The agaricales in modern taxonomy. 3rd ed. J. Gramer, Vaduz. 912.

Wilkinson, D. M and Dichinson, N. M. 1995. Metal resistance in trees: the role of mycorrhizae. Oikos. 72:298-300.

Wu, L. and Antonovis, J. 1975. Zn and Cu uptake by *Agrostis stolonifera*, tolerant to both Zn and Cu. New Phytol. 75:231-237.

Heavy Metal Pollution and Mycorrhiza : **57-85**
Authors : Prof. G. D. Sharma and Dr. Tali Ajungla
Today & Tomorrow's Printers and Publishers. New Delhi-110 002

Chapter 4

Heavy metals and metabolic activities of ectomycorrhizal roots:

Introduction

The enzyme activity is often used as an index of microbial activity as well as an index of soil fertility. Any particular enzyme, and its overall activity is often a complex of activities associated with various biotic and abiotic components e.g. proliferating cells, latent cells, cell debris, clay minerals, humic colloids and the soil aqueous phase (Burns, 1982). Enzymes are biologically significant in soil mainly due to their participation in cycling of nutrients which influence nutrient availability to plants. Microorganisms, active roots and dead cells are the principal sources of soil enzymes (Tiwari *et al.,* 1988).

Dehydrogenase, urease and phosphatase are important soil enzymes. The measurement of dehydrogenase activity provides an index of the metabolic activity in a soil. Urease and phosphatases are involved in transformation of nitrogen and phosphorus respectively. Activity of these enzymes correlates with the microbial activity. Dehydrogenase activity in soil provides correlative information on the biological activity on microbial population. Microbial biomass and dehydrogenase activity have been observed to be influenced by rhizosphere of the host plant (Speir *et al.,* 1980). Urease activity generally correlates with organic matter content. Various factors such as pH, moisture content, temperature and number of microorganisms affect the urease activity in soil (Jha *et al.,* 1992). Phosphatase is thought to be directly related to the level of organic phosphorus in the soil. Acid phosphatase is responsible for hydrolysis of organic phosphorus in the soil (Rogers *et al.,* 1942). Therefore, the activity of these enzymes is significant in P-cycling and in plant nutrition. Phosphatases are also produced by ectomycorrhizal fungi (Dighton, 1983). Acid phosphatase activity and fungal mantle mycelium hydrolyse the complex organic phosphorus which improves the nutrient uptake.

Root surface phospahtase may be more important in the organic phosphorus mobilization and making it available to the plants (Antibus *et al.,*1992). The number of mycorrhizal rootlets and fungal mycelium associated with them is determined by the specific mycobiont is important. The root surface phosphatase activity has its own relationship with mycorrhizal association and P-uptake (Dodd *et al.,*1987).

The number of mycorrhizal rootlets and fungal mycelium associated with them as determined by the specific mycobiont is important. Variation in the efficiency of mycorrhizae for metabolic activities and uptake of N, P and K may depend on the specific mycorrhizal fungi. The benefit of mycorrhizae for improving status of trees are largely related to hyphal net of extrametrical mycelia for mycorrhizal fungi in the soil providing a large surface for absorption and uptake of nutrients (Rousseau *et al.*, 1994). Most of the studies have shown that the enzyme activity was subjected to seasonal variation.

Heavy metals and dehydrogenase activity:

Dehydrogenase was apparently less at high concentration of heavy metals. Inoculation of mycorrhizal fungi to seedlings increased the activities of dehydrogenase. Highest activity was observed during summer and minimum was observed during winter months. In all the four seasons, the dehydrogenase activity was more in the root region than in rhizospheric soil. The seasonal fluctuations followed divergent pattern during the year. During summer months, dehydrogenase activity remained almost constant, but after September it decreased considerably and reached its minimum and during this period soil temperature and moisture of the soil were also recorded lowest. During winter and spring months, variation was low. After the rainy month of May, the enzyme activity started to increase gradually and reached its peak in August. The heavy metals inhibited the activity of dehydrogenase significantly more in non-mycorrhizal seedlings than mycorrhizal ones. It could be informed that adverse affect due to heavy metals was severe and prolonged in non-mycorrhizal seedlings. In *Boletus* inoculated seedlings, Cu and Zn did not reduce the dehydrogenase acitivty significantly both in rhizospheric soil and in mycorrhizal root region (Figs. 1-6 & 7-12). Among the four ectomycorrhizal fungi, *Scleroderma aurantium* treated roots showed the least seasonal variation but had highest activity (Fig 13-18).

Fig.1-6 Dehydrogenase Activity on Root Surface Inoculated with *Boletus sp.*

Formazan released mg/g dry wt/24 h

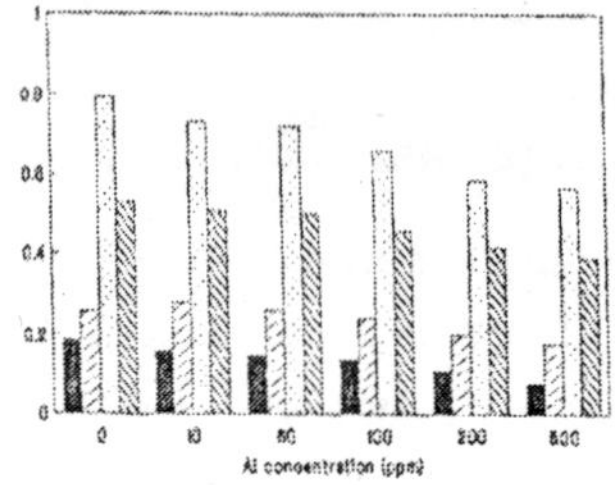

Fig.1 winter spring summer autumn

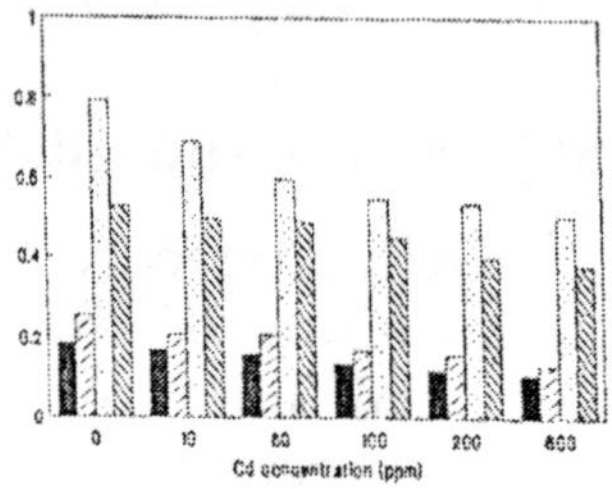

Fig.2 winter spring summer autumn

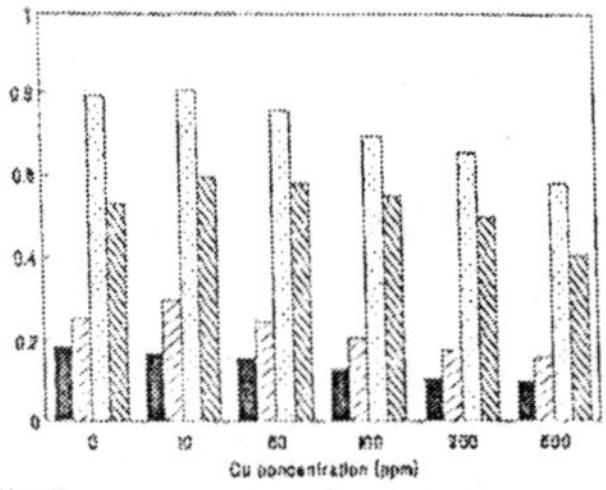

Fig.3 winter spring summer autumn

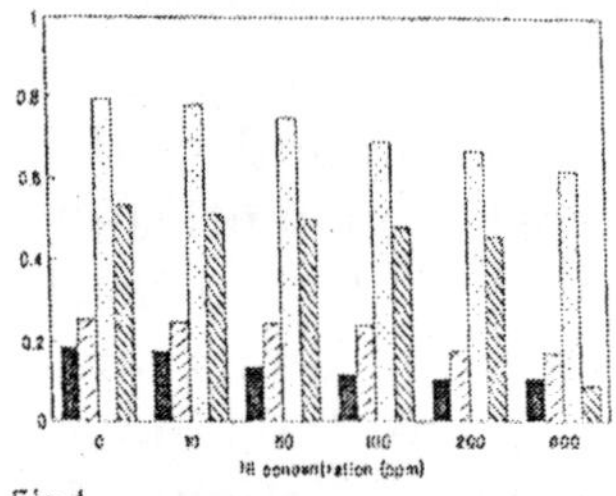

Fig.4 winter spring summer autumn

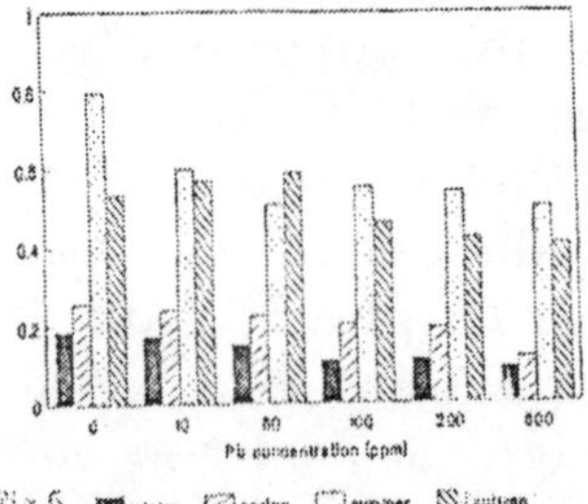

Fig.5 winter spring summer autumn

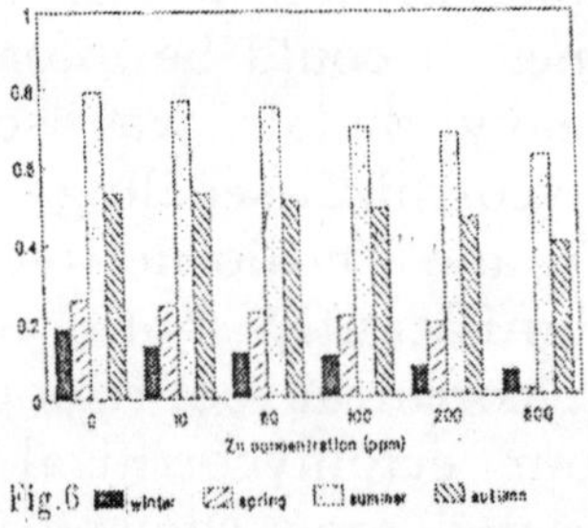

Fig.6 winter spring summer autumn

Fig. 7–12 Dehydrogenase Activity on rhizospheric Soil Inoculated with *Boletus sp.*

Formazan released mg/g dry wt/24 h

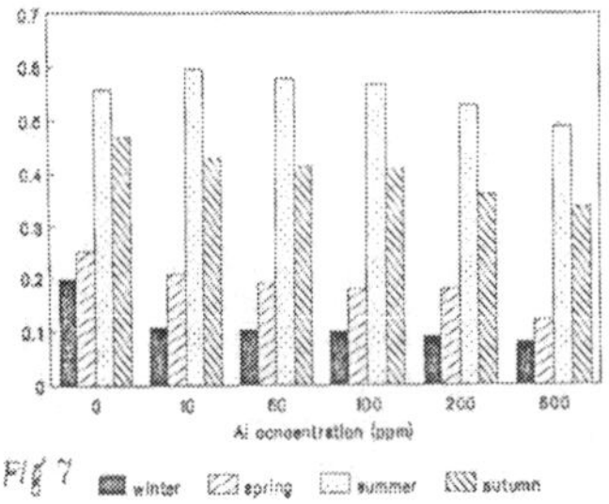

Fig. 7

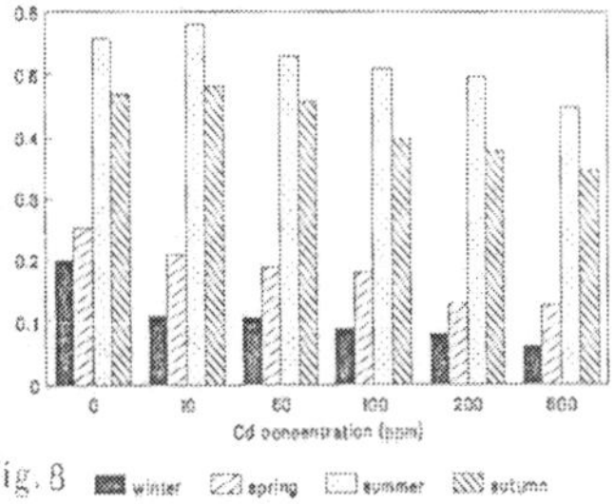

Fig. 8

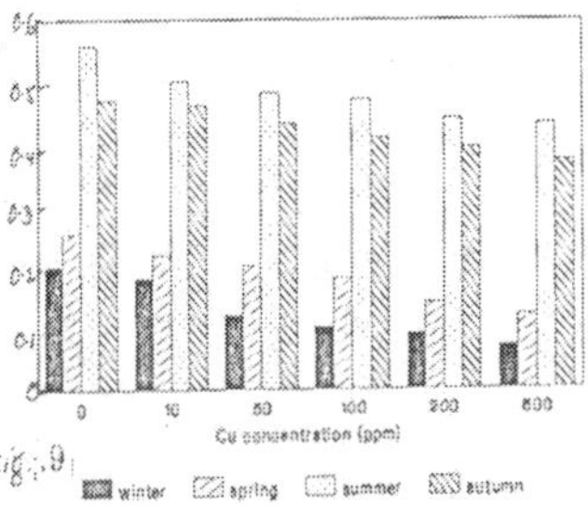

Fig. 9

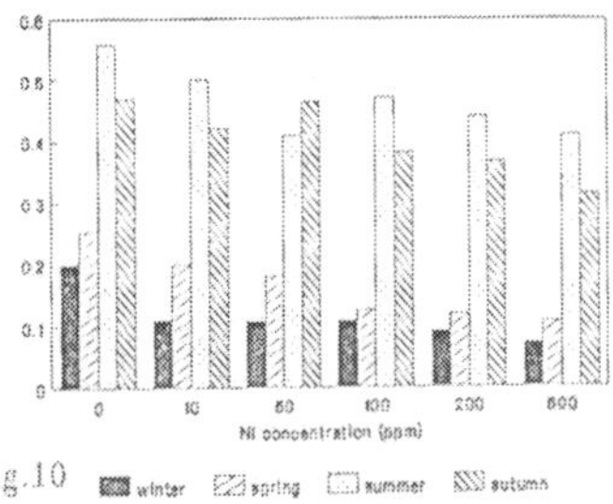

Fig. 10

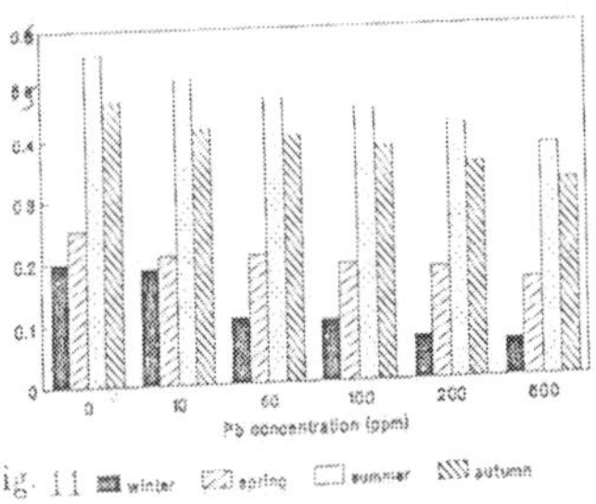

Fig. 11

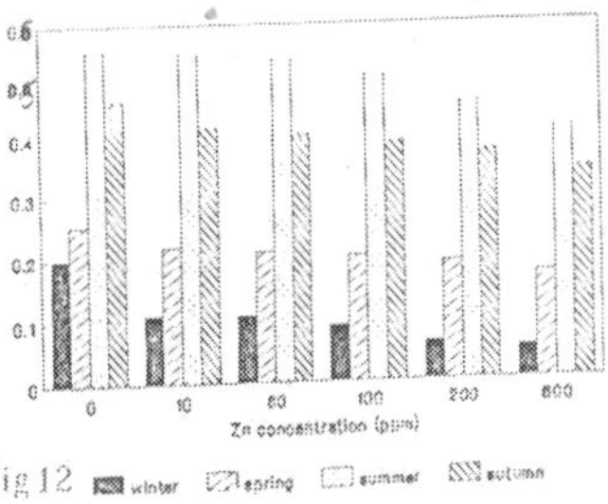

Fig. 12

Fig.13–18 Dehydrogenase Activity on Root Surface Inoculated with *S.aurantium*

Formazan released mg/g dry wt/24 h

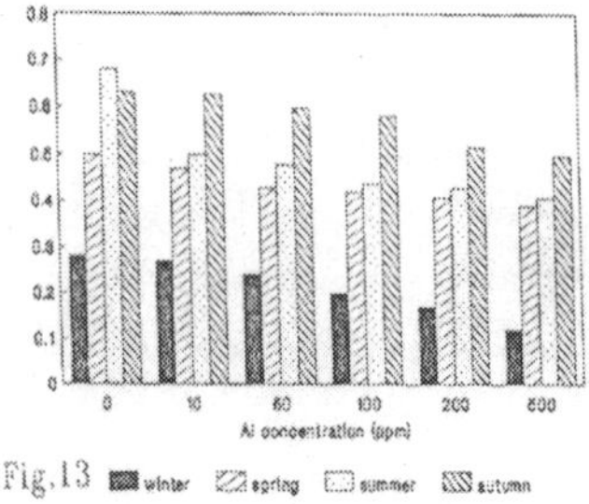

Fig.13

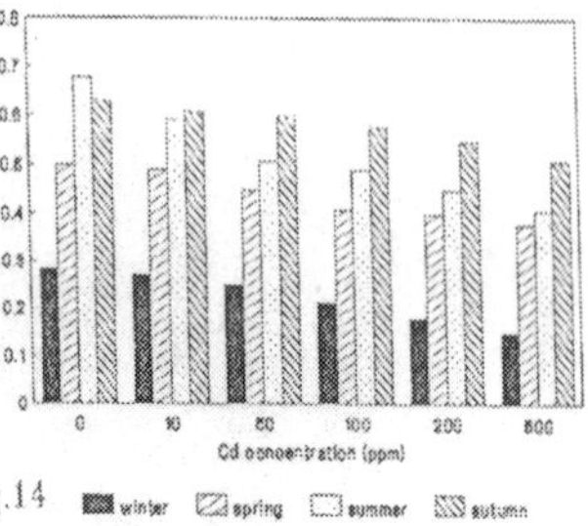

Fig.14

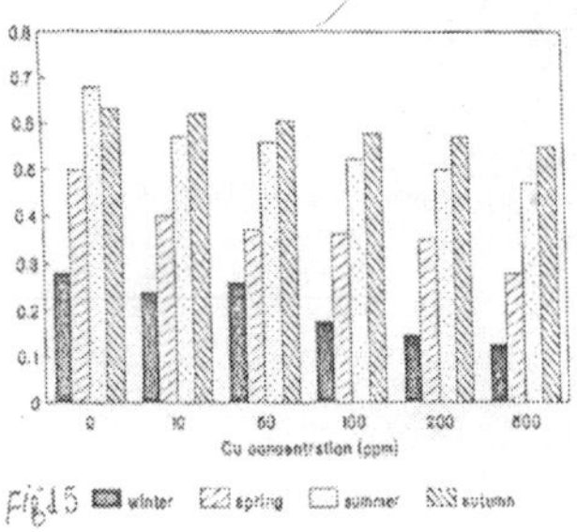

Fig.15

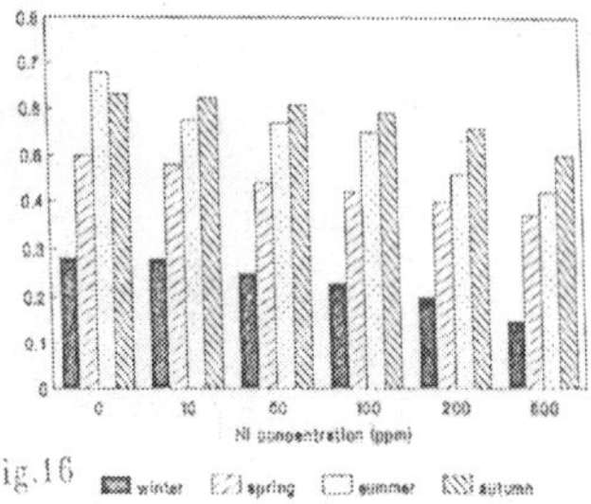

Fig.16

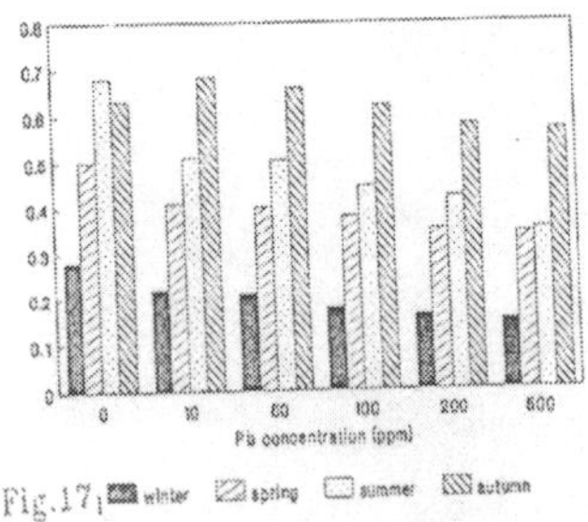

Fig.17

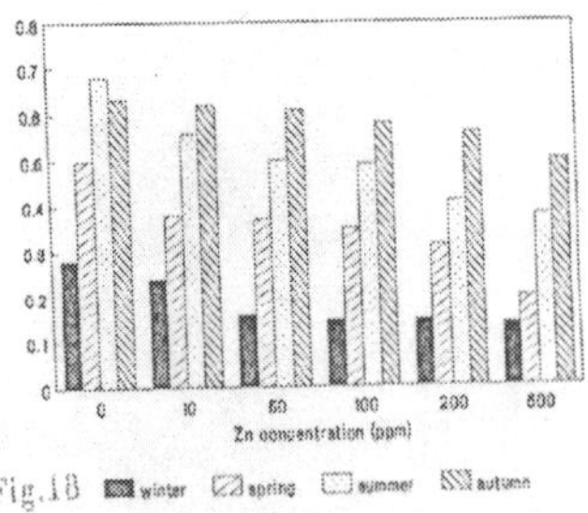

Fig.18

Fig.19-24 Dehydrogenase Activity on Root Surface Inoculated with *S.luteus*

Formazan released mg/g dry wt/24 h

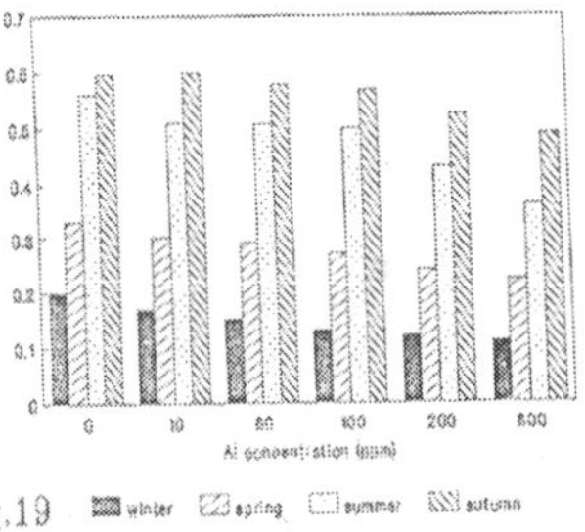

Fig.19

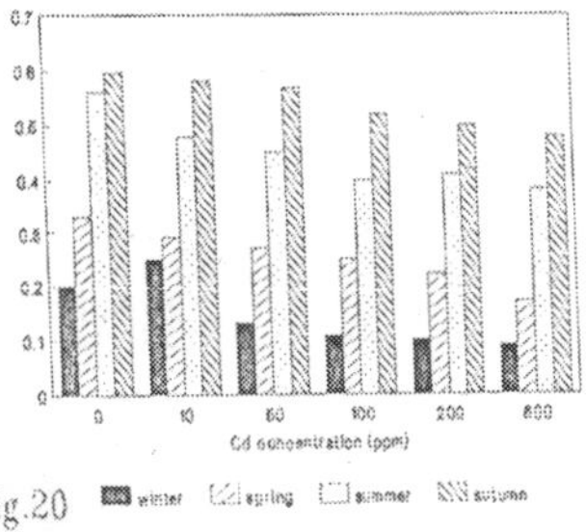

Fig.20

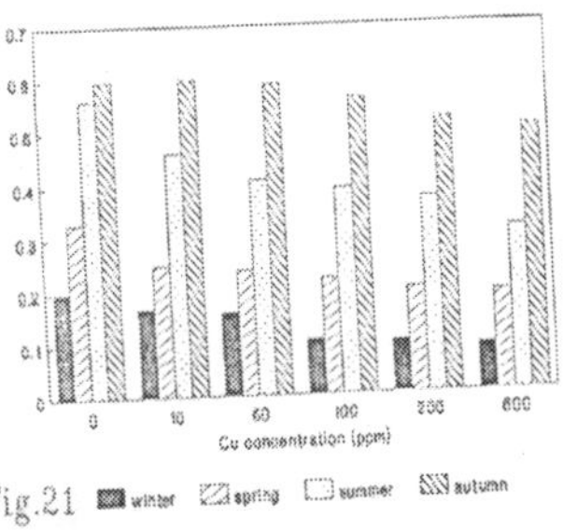

Fig.21

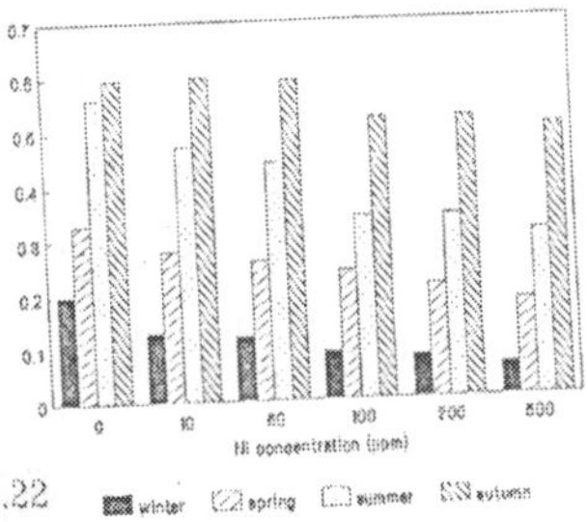

Fig.22

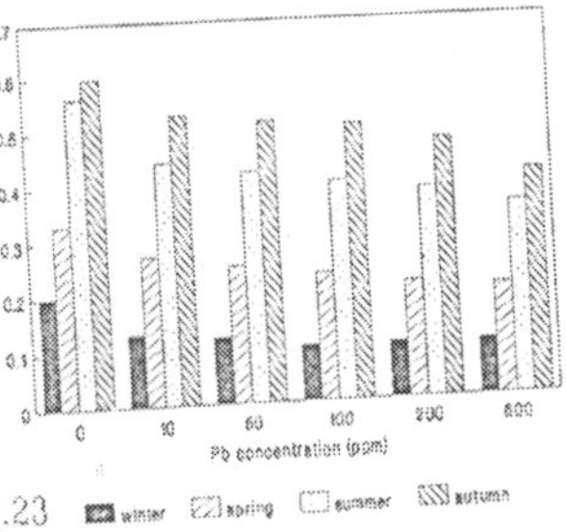

Fig.23

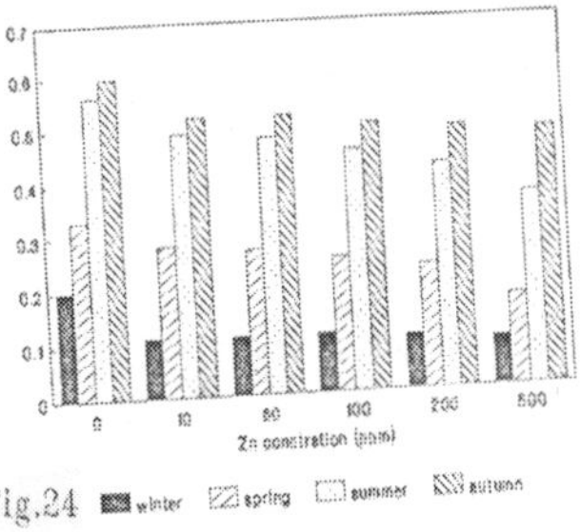

Fig.24

Fig. 25-30 Dehydrogenase Activity in rhizospheric Soil Inoculated with *S. luteus*

Formazan released mg/g dry wt/24 h

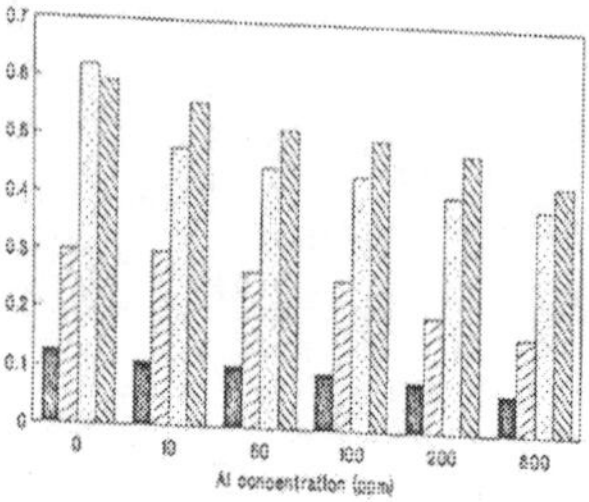

Fig 25 winter spring summer autumn

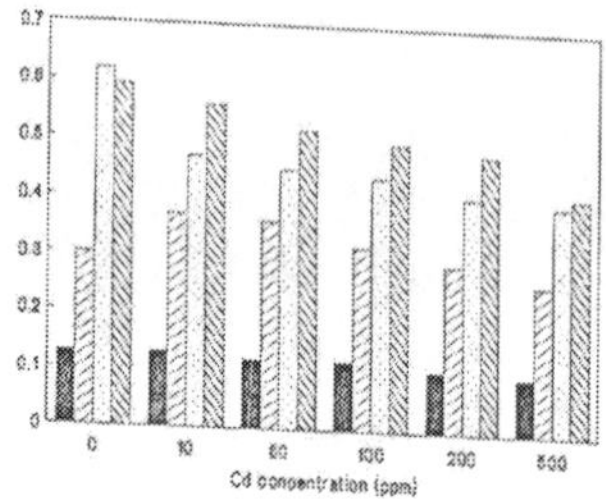

Fig.26 winter spring summer autumn

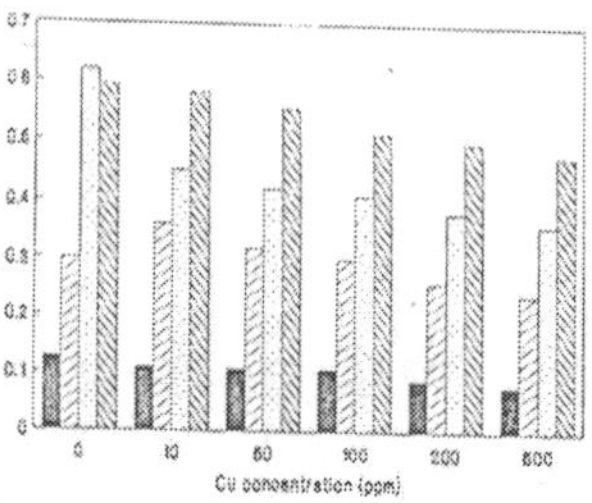

Fig.27 winter spring summer autumn

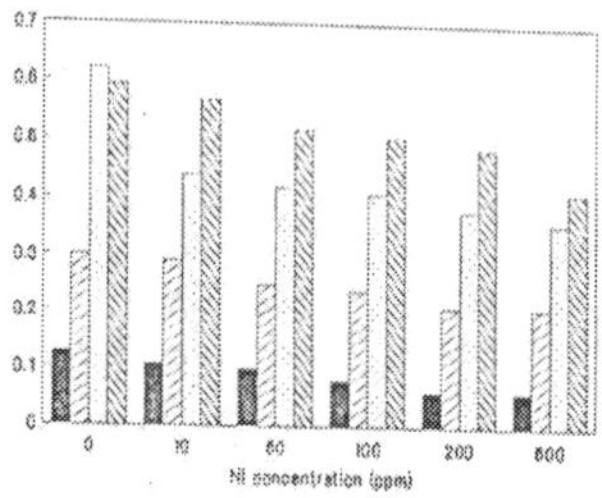

Fig.28 winter spring summer autumn

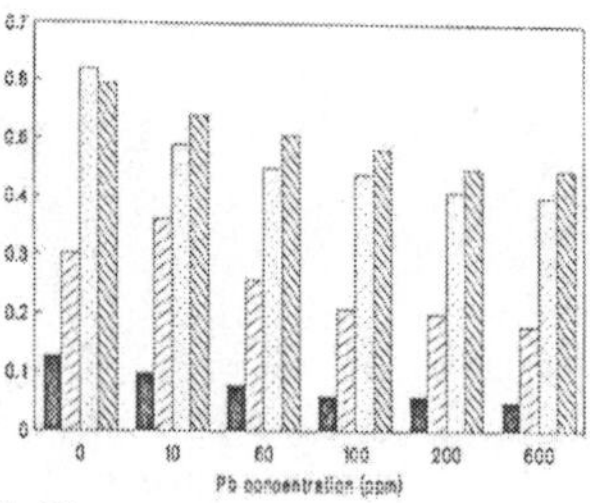

Fig.29 winter spring summer autumn

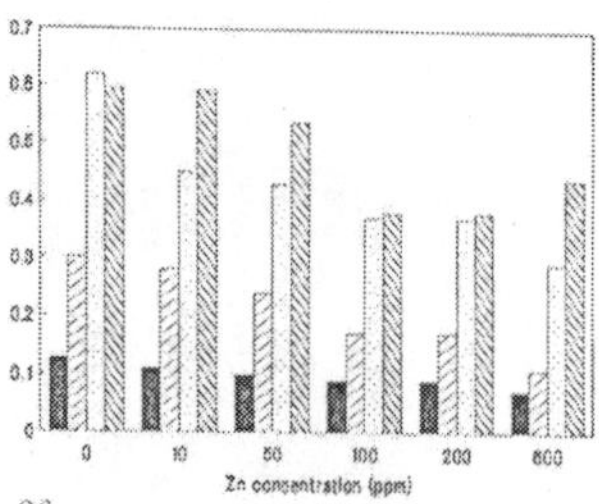

Fig.30 winter spring summer autumn

Fig. 31-36 : Dehydrogenase Activity in Root Surface Inoculated with Mixed mycobionts

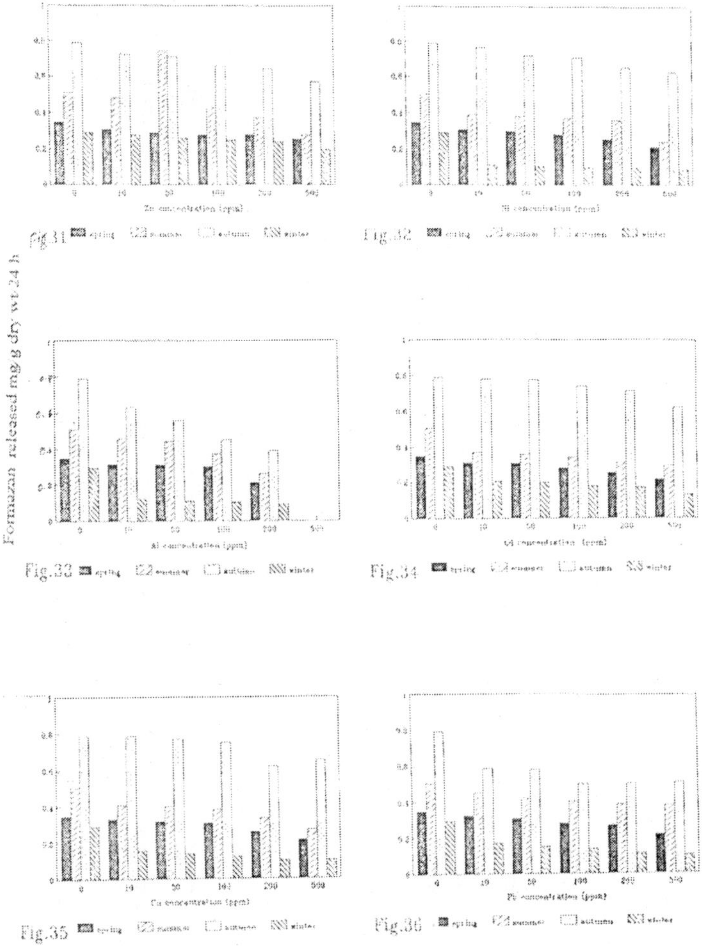

Fig.37–42 Dehydrogenase Activity on rhizospheric Soil Inoculated with mixed mycobionts

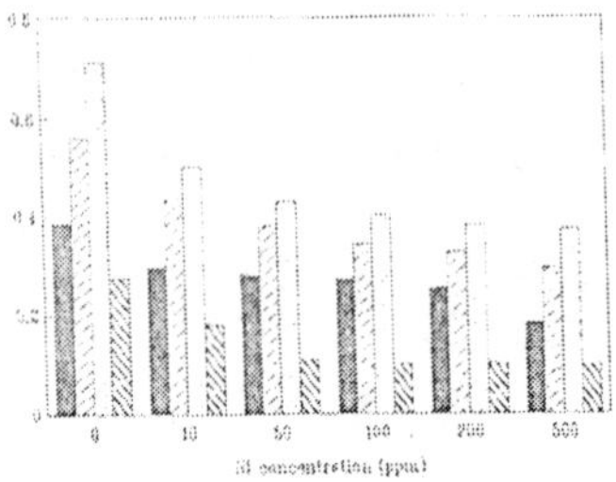

Fig.37 spring summer autumn winter

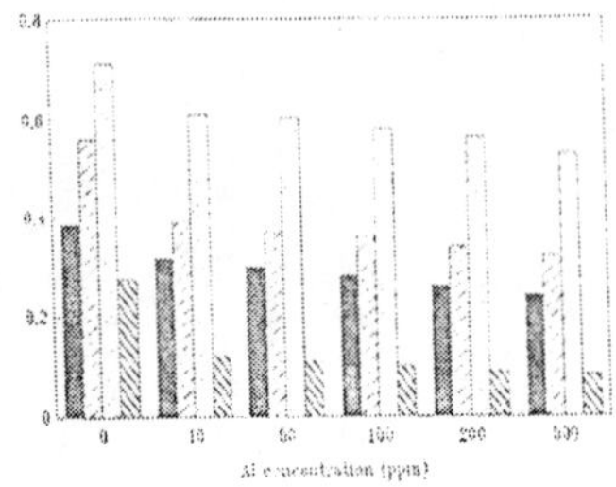

Fig.38 spring summer autumn winter

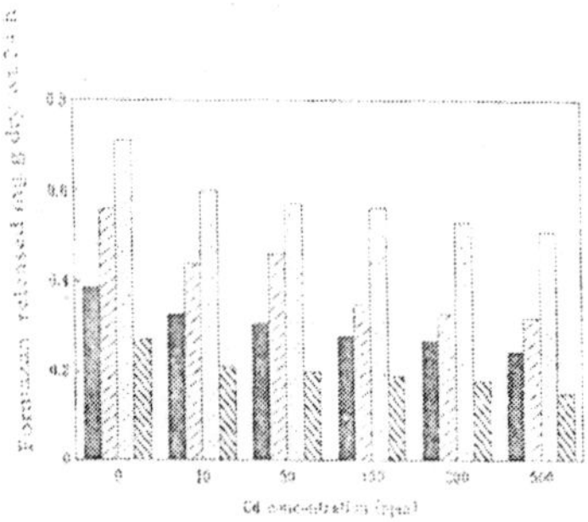

Fig.39 spring summer autumn winter

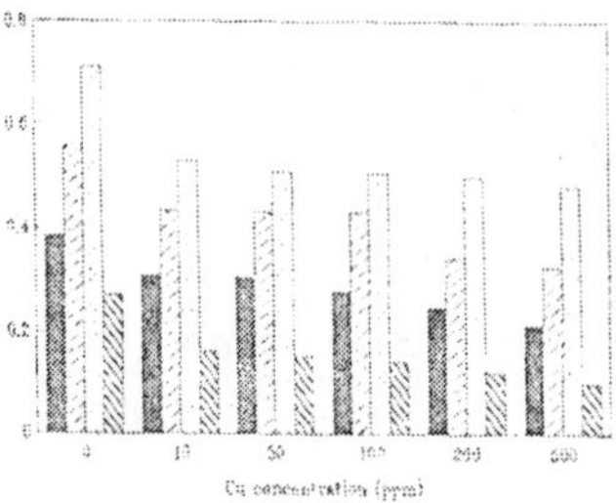

Fig.40 spring summer autumn winter

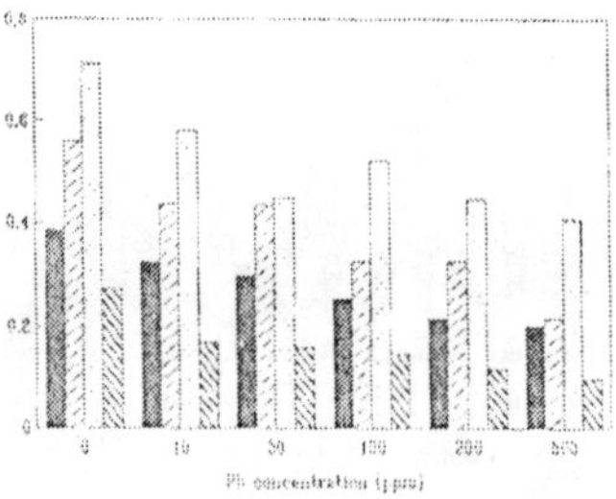

Fig.41 spring summer autumn winter

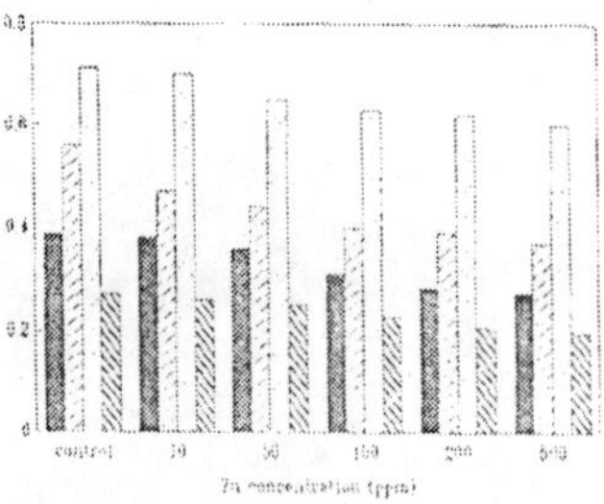

Fig.42 spring autumn summer winter

Fig.43-48 Urease Activity on Non-mycorrhizal Root Surface

NH$_4$-N released mg/g dry wt/3h

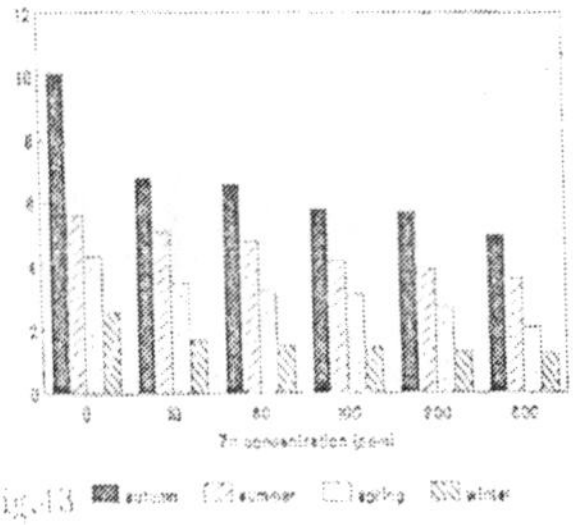

Fig.43

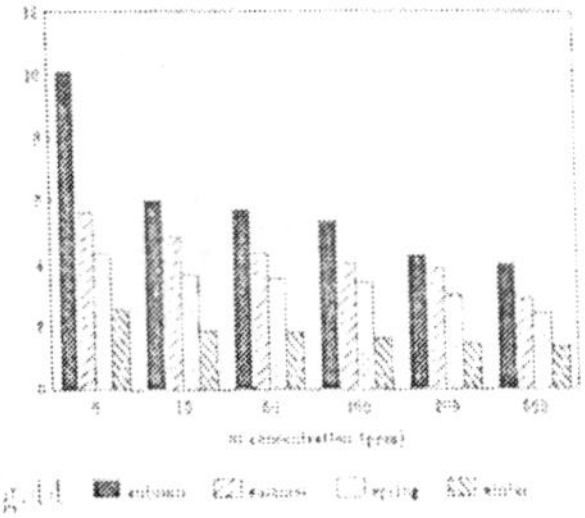

Fig.44

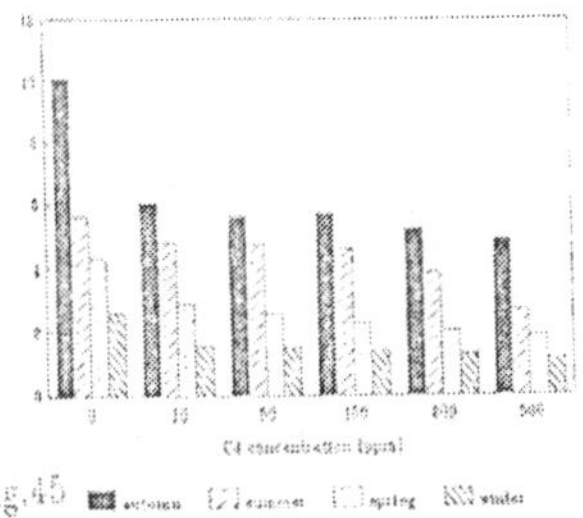

Fig.45

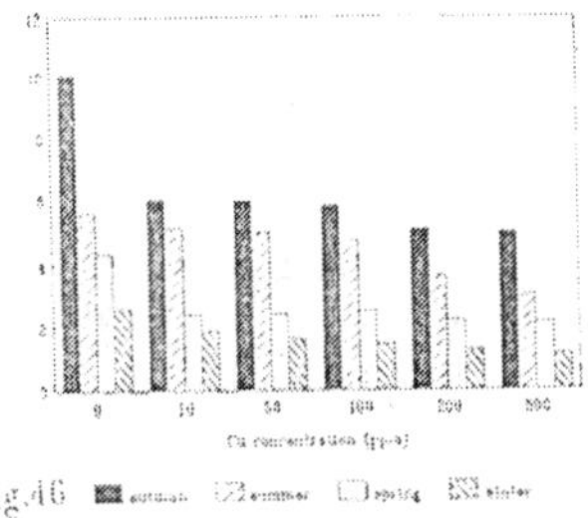

Fig.46

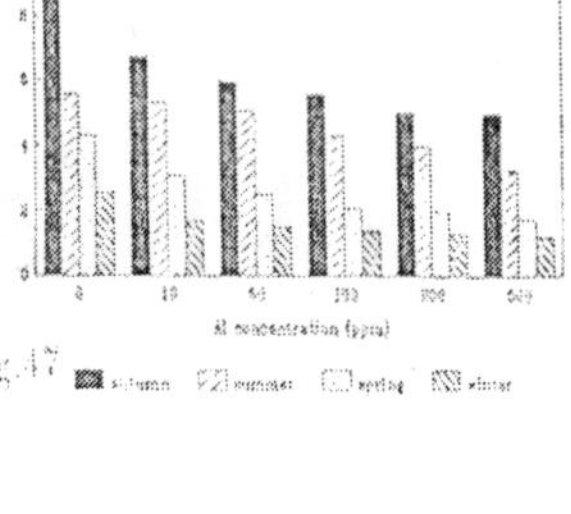

Fig.47

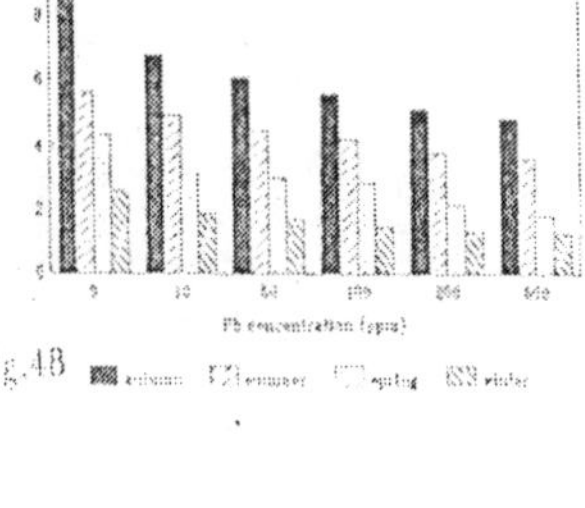

Fig.48

Fig.49–54 Urease Activity on Root Surface Inoculated with mixed mycobionts

NH$_4$-N released mg/g dry wt/3h

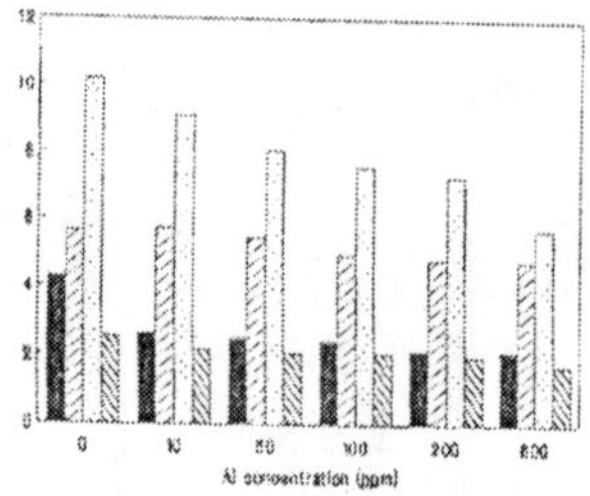

Fig.49 spring summer autumn winter

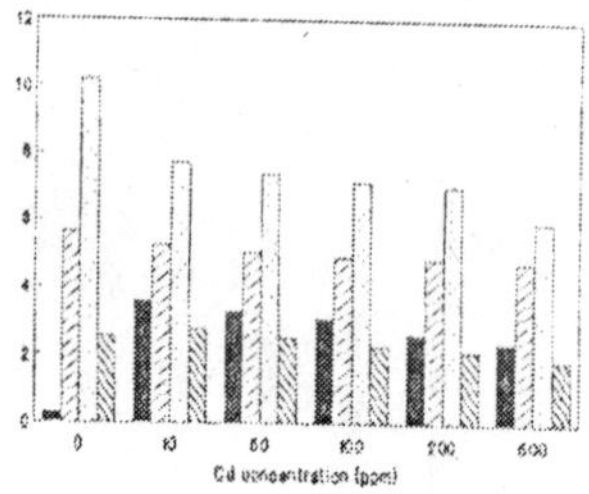

Fig.50 spring summer autumn winter

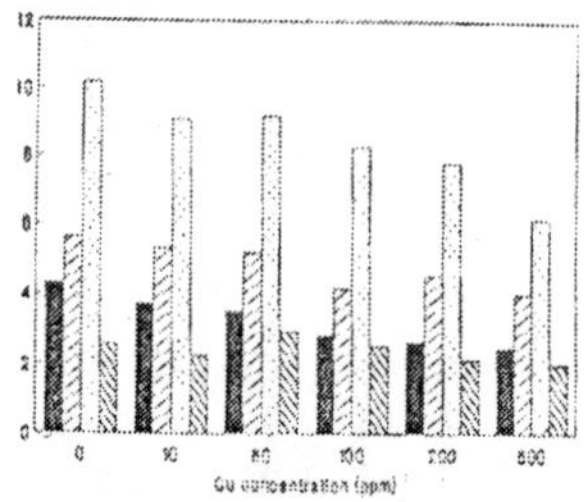

Fig.51 spring summer autumn winter

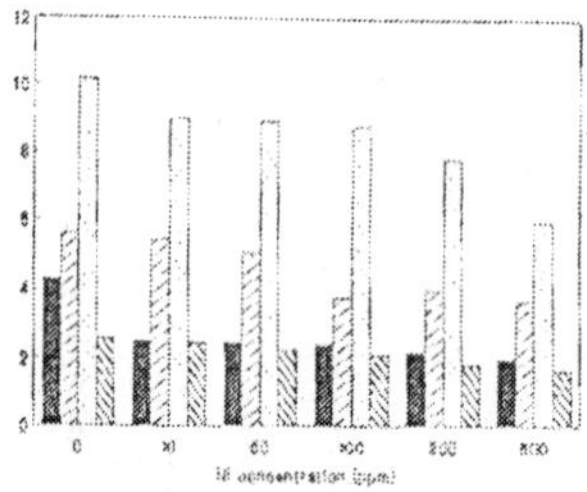

Fig.52 spring summer autumn winter

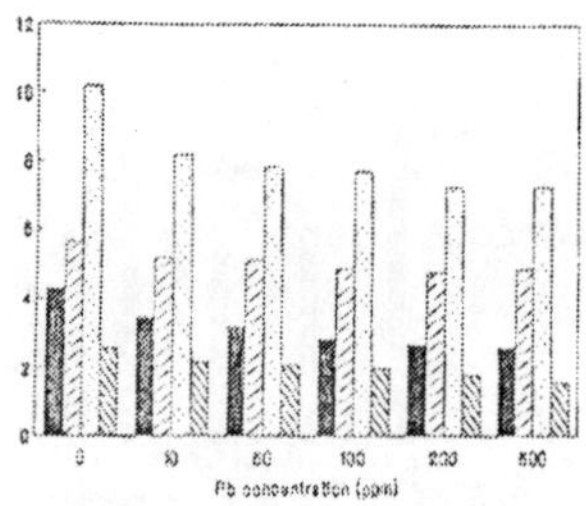

Fig.53 spring summer autumn winter

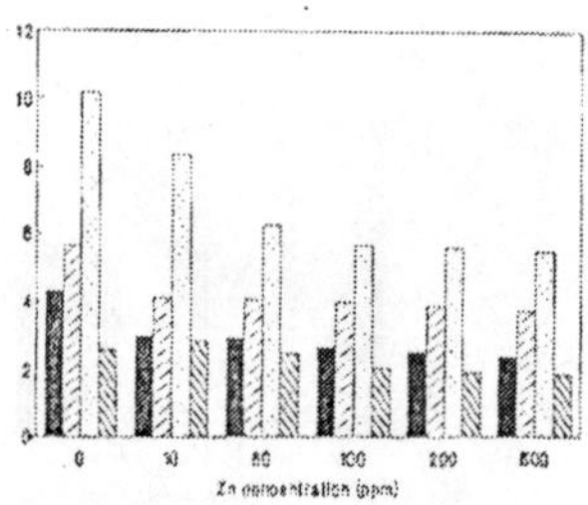

Fig.54 spring summer autumn winter

Fig. 55-60 : Urease Activity in rhizospheric Soil Inoculated with mixed mycobionts

NH_4^+-N released mg/g dry wt/3h

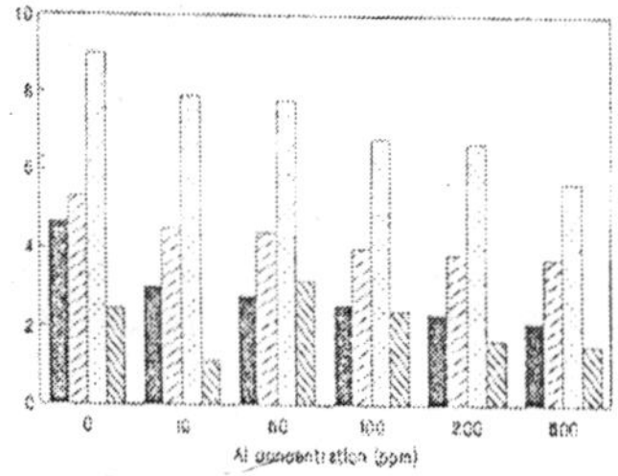

Fig.55 spring summer autumn winter

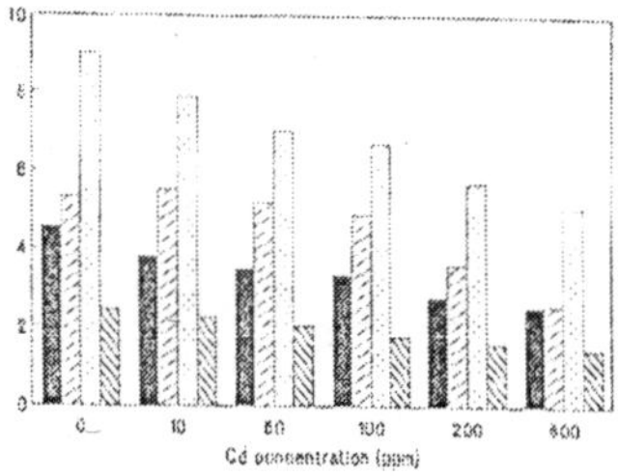

Fig.56 spring summer autumn winter

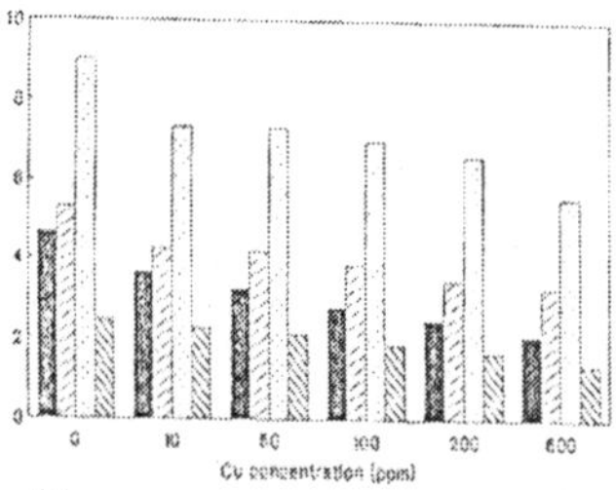

Fig.57 spring summer autumn winter

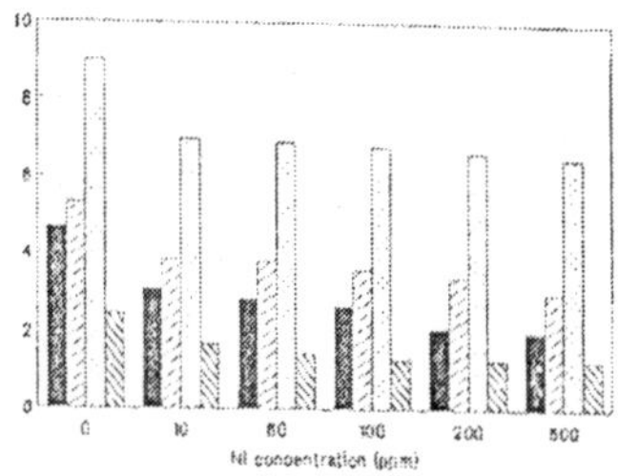

Fig.58 spring summer autumn winter

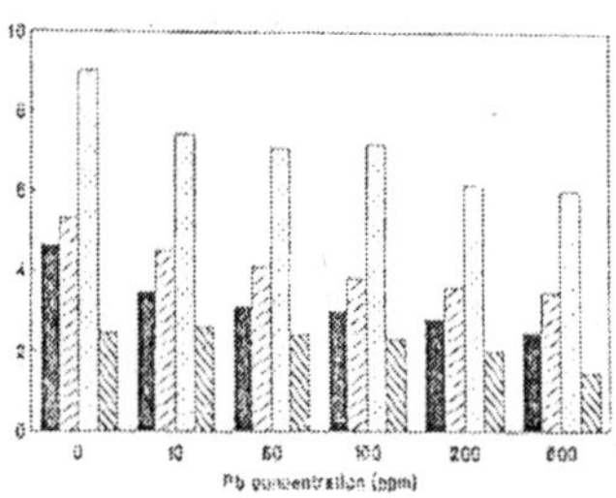

Fig.59 spring summer autumn winter

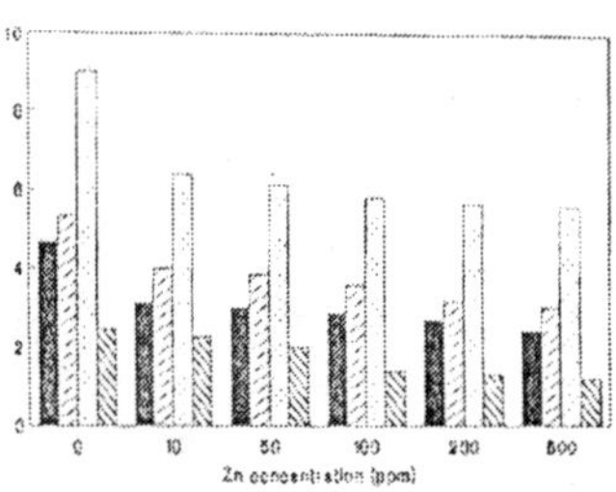

Fig.60 spring summer autumn winter

Fig. 61-66 Urease activity in rhizospheric soil Incoulated with *S. aurantium*

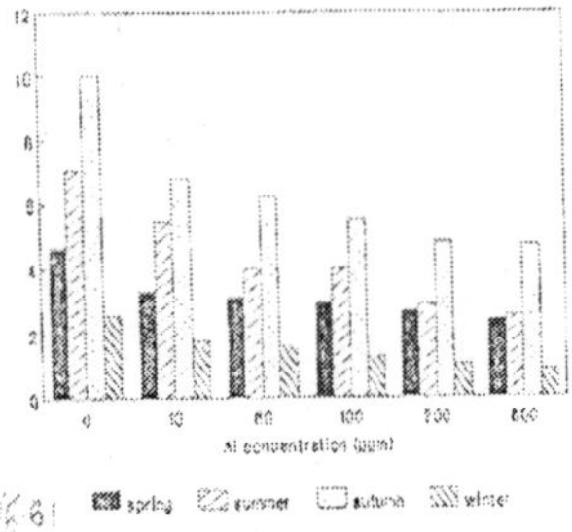

Fig 61

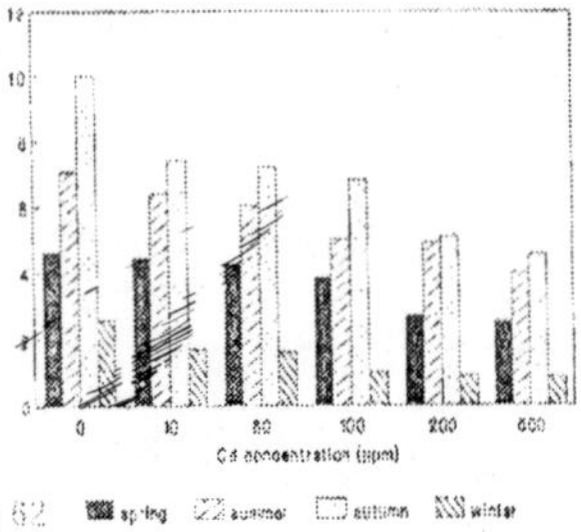

Fig 62

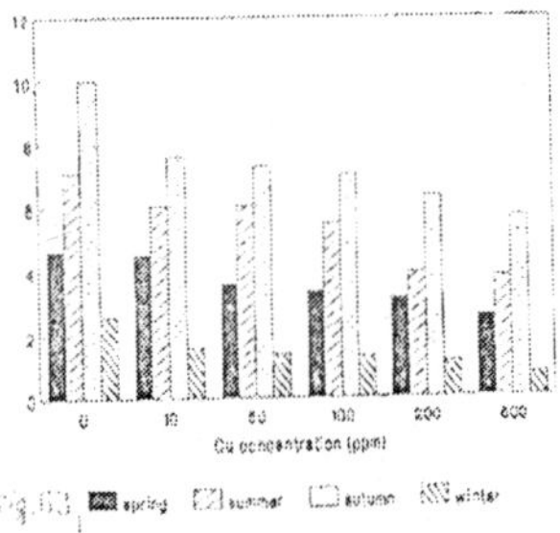

Fig 63

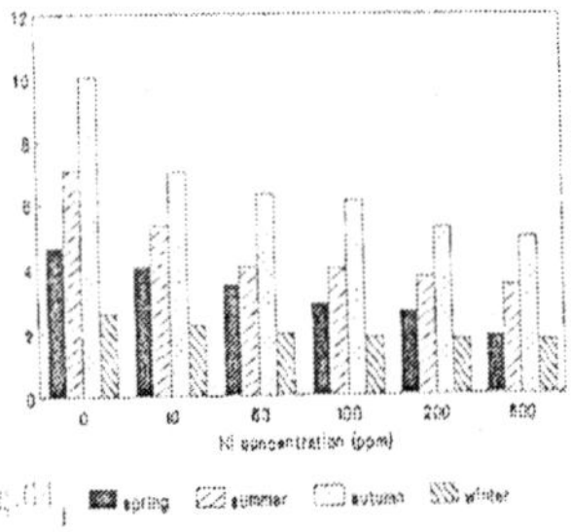

Fig 64

NH_4^+-N released mg/g dry wt/3h

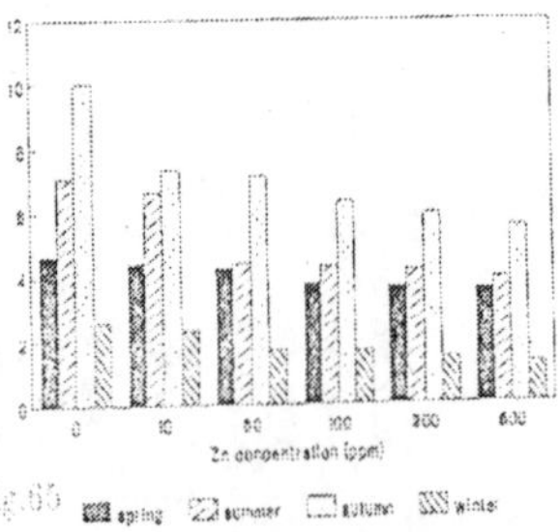

Fig 65

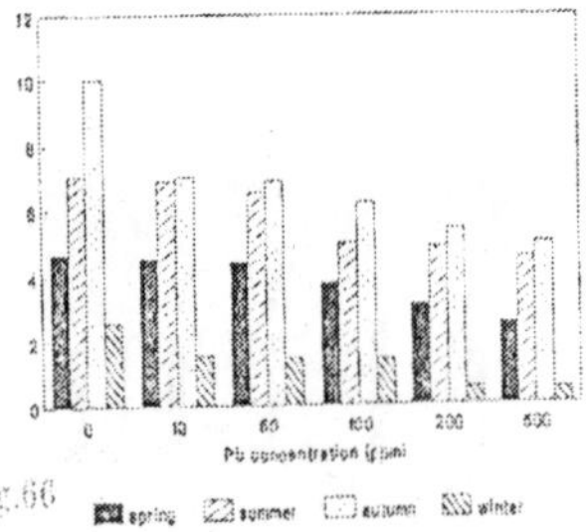

Fig 66

Fig. 67-72 Urease Activity in Non-Mycorrhizal rhizospheric soil

NH_4-N released mg/g dry wt/3h

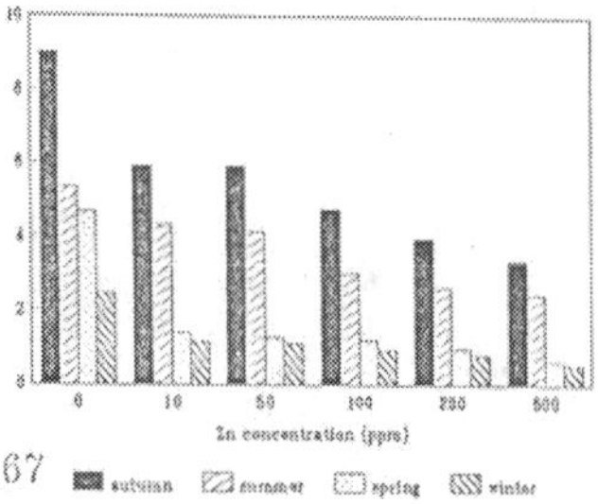

Fig.67

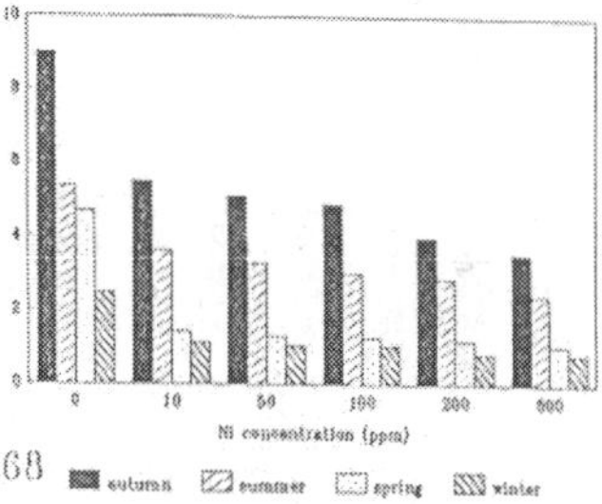

Fig.68

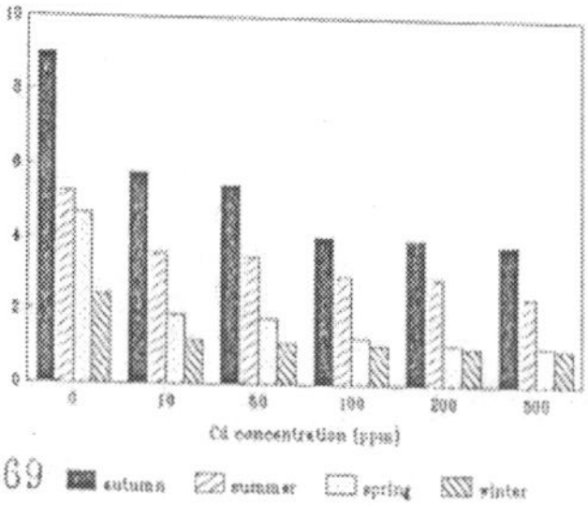

Fig.69

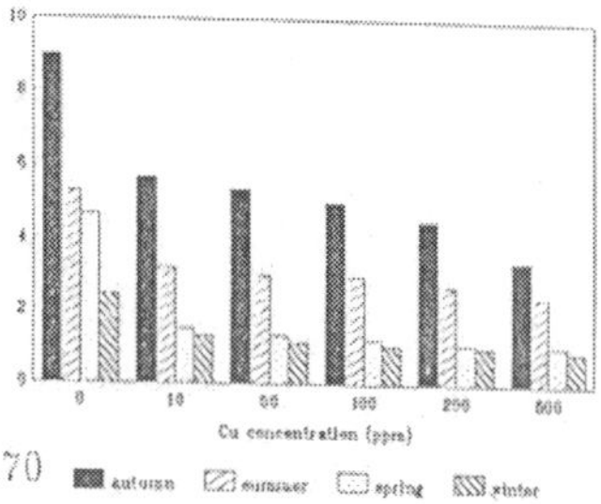

Fig.70

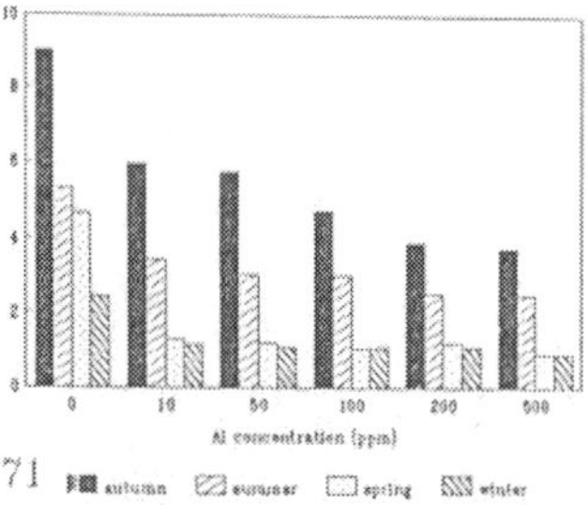

Fig.71

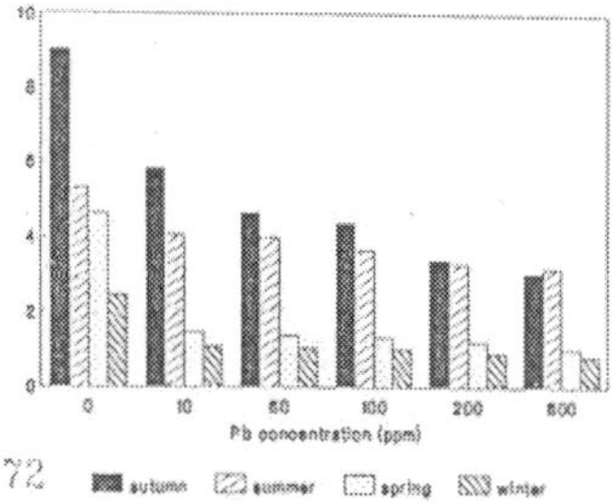

Fig.72

Fig. 73-78 Phosphatase activity in Root Surface Inoculated with Mixed Mycobionts

... mixed mycobionts

mazan released mg g dry wt. 24 h

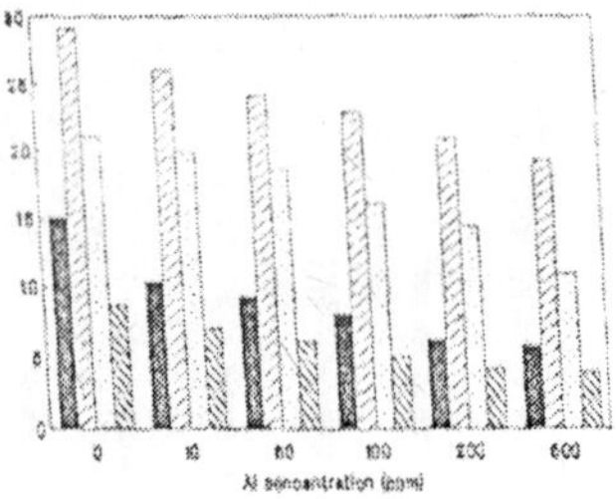

Fig.73 spring autumn summer winter

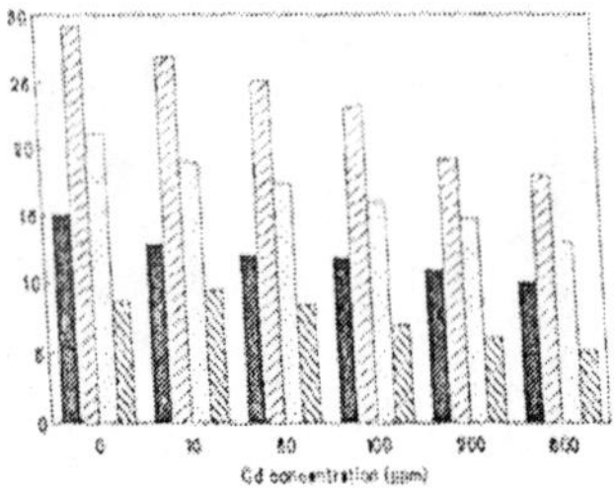

Fig.74 spring autumn summer winter

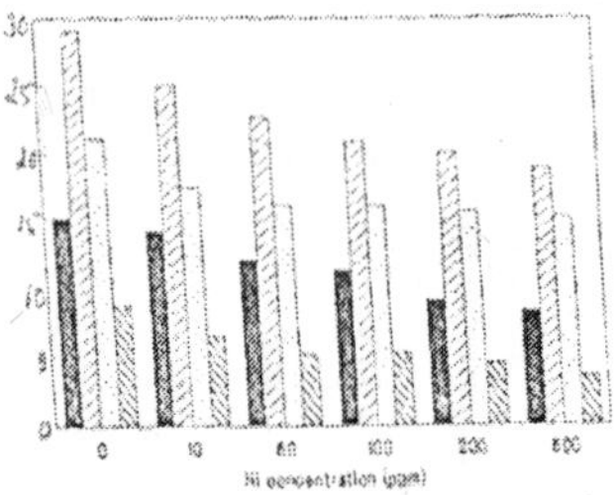

Fig.75 spring autumn summer winter

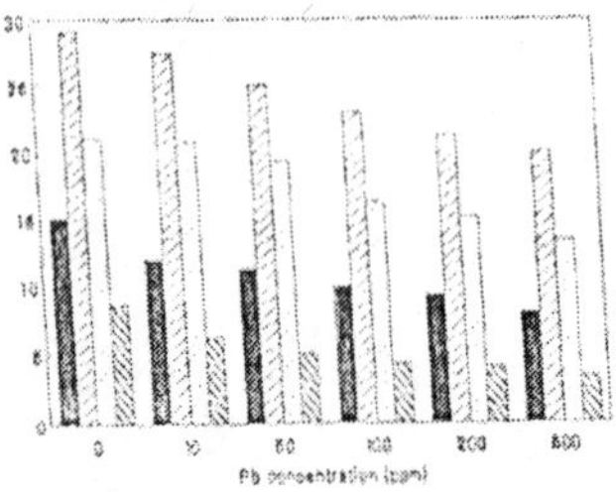

Fig.76 spring autumn summer winter

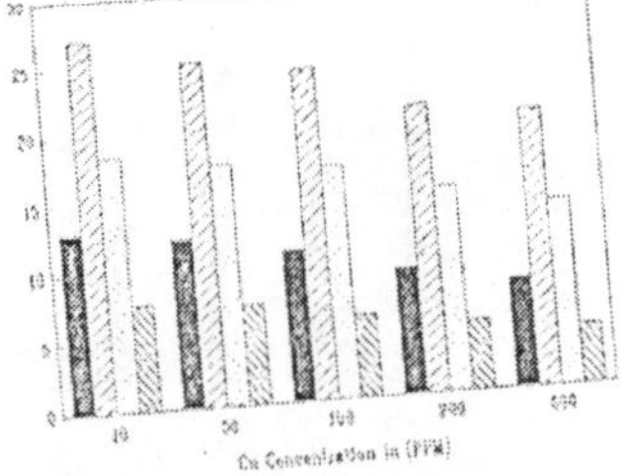

Fig.77 spring autumn summer winter

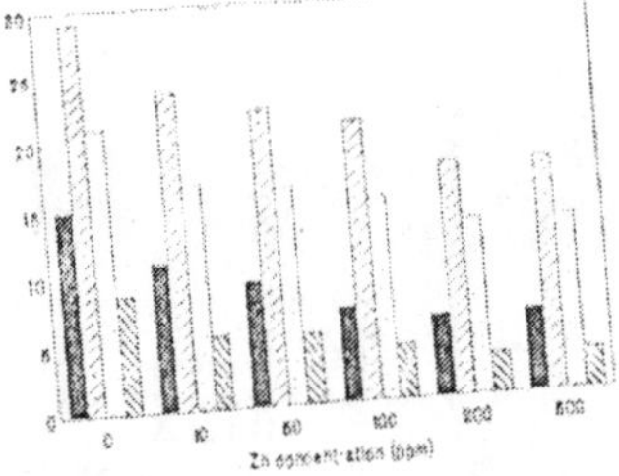

Fig.78 spring autumn summer winter

Fig. 79-84 Phosphatase Activity in rizospheric soil Inoculated with *S. aurantium*

P-nitrophenol released mg/g dry wt/h

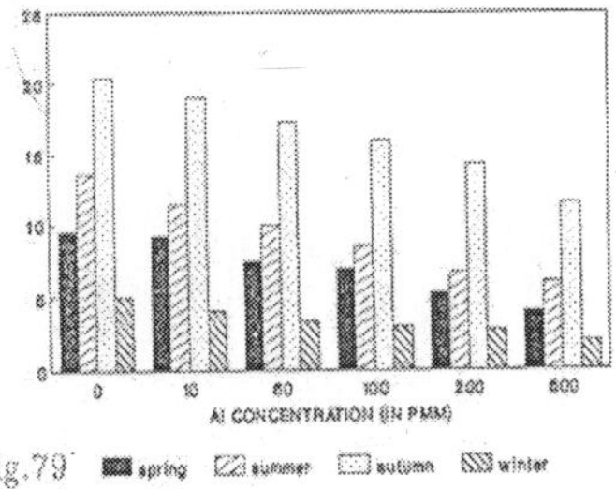

Fig.79

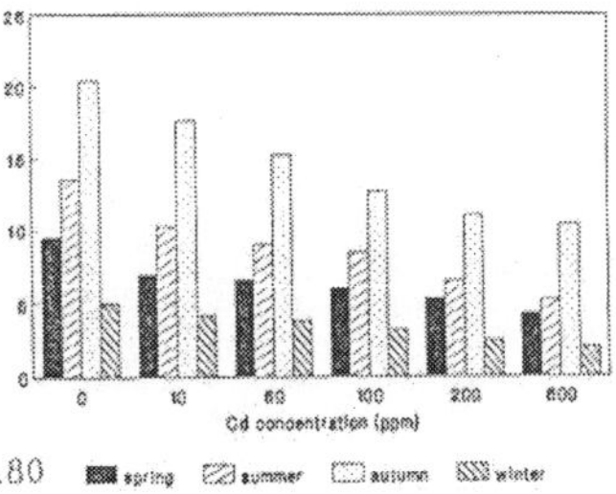

Fig.80

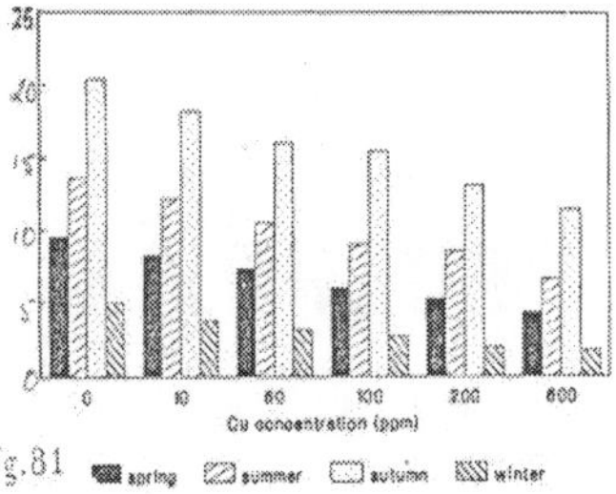

Fig.81

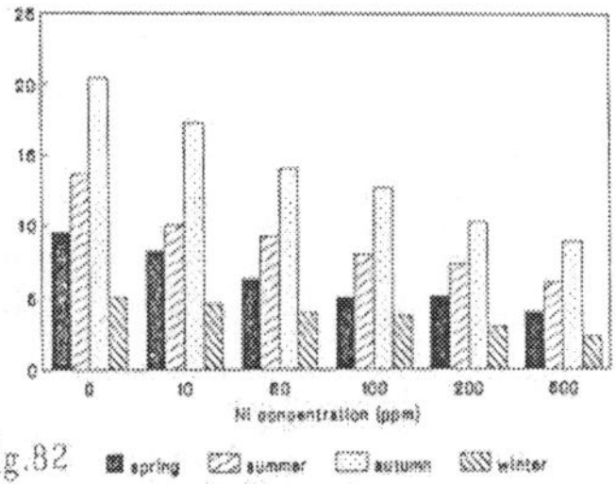

Fig.82

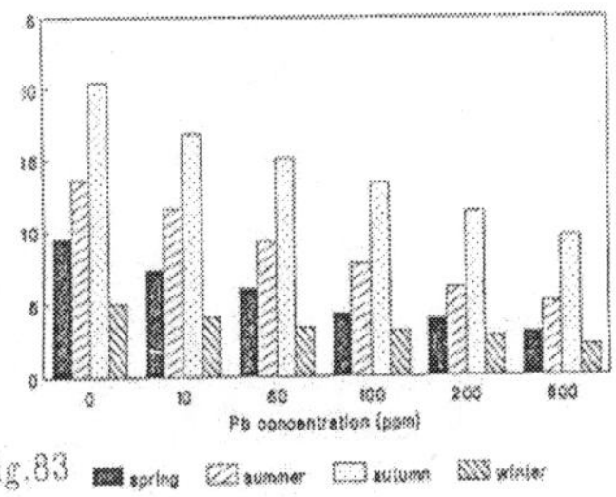

Fig.83

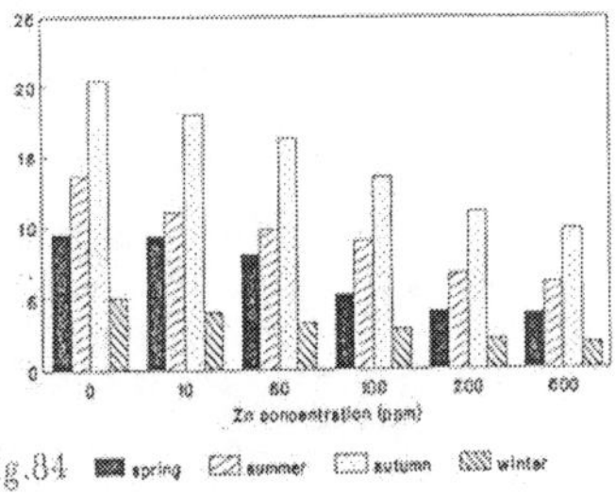

Fig.84

Fig.85–90 Phosphatase Activity on Root Surface Inoculated with *Boletus sp.*

P-nitrophenol released mg/g dry wt/h

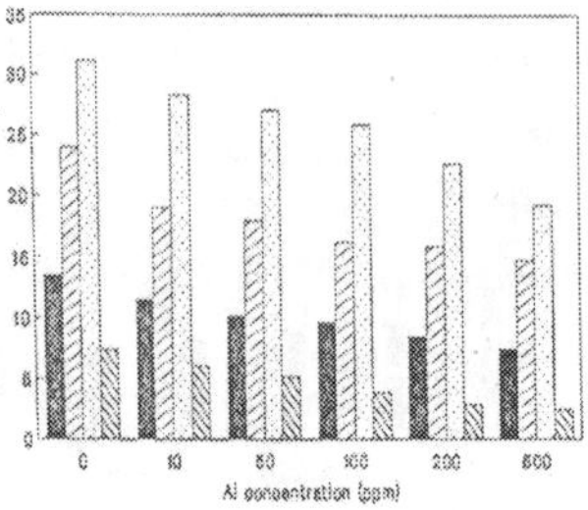

Fig.85 spring summer autumn winter

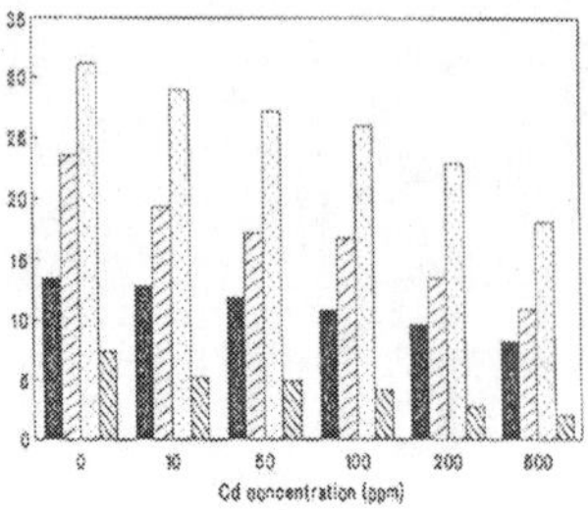

Fig.86 spring summer autumn winter

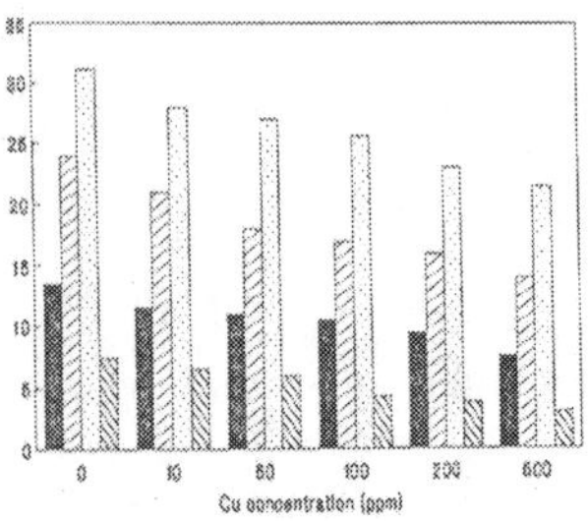

Fig.87 spring summer autumn winter

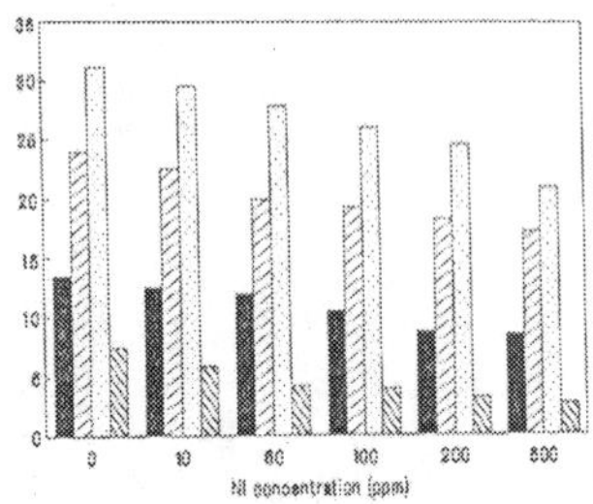

Fig.88 spring summer autumn winter

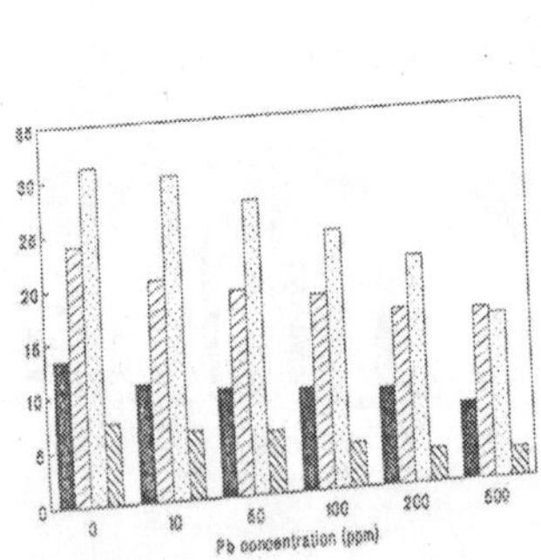

Fig.89 spring summer autumn winter

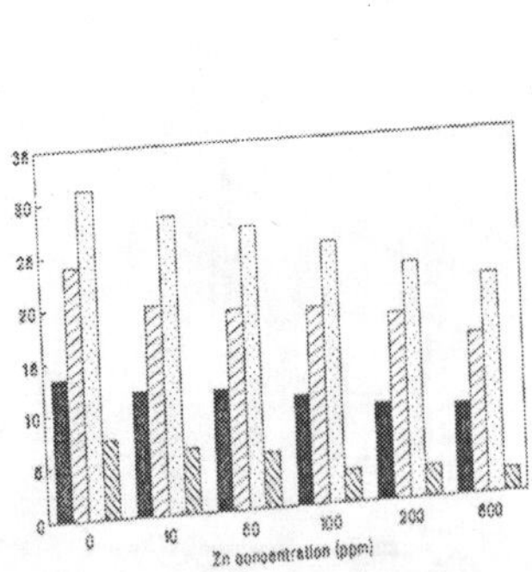

Fig.90 spring summer autumn winter

Fig. 91-96 Phosphatase Activity in rhizospheric Soil Inoculated with *Botatus sp.*

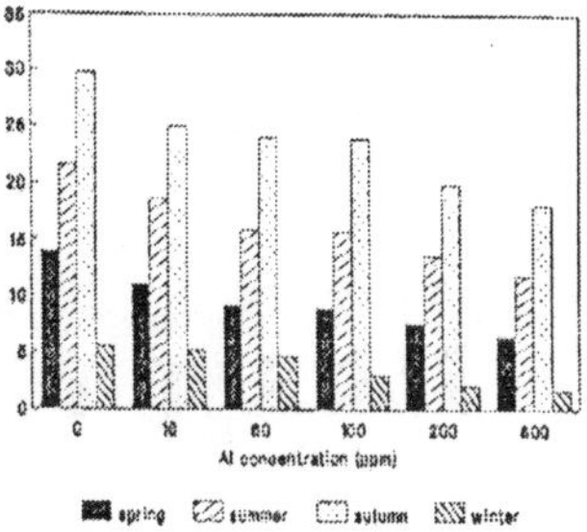

Fig.91

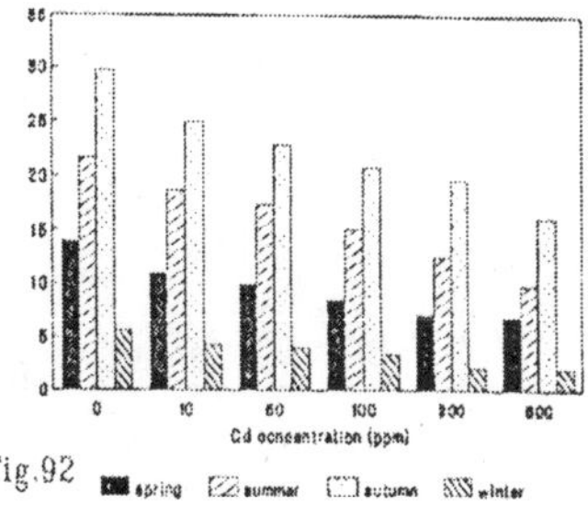

Fig.92

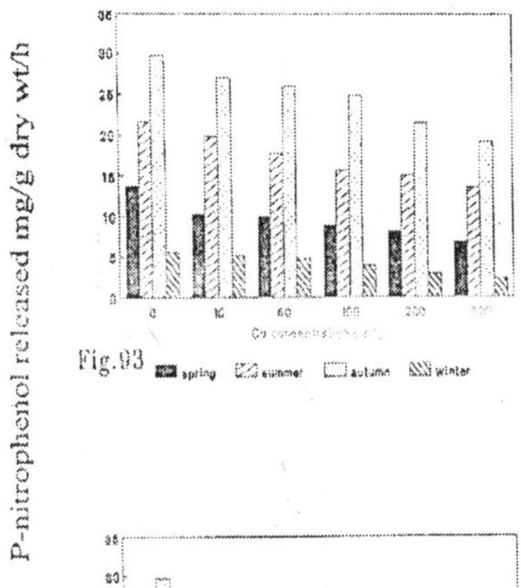

Fig.93

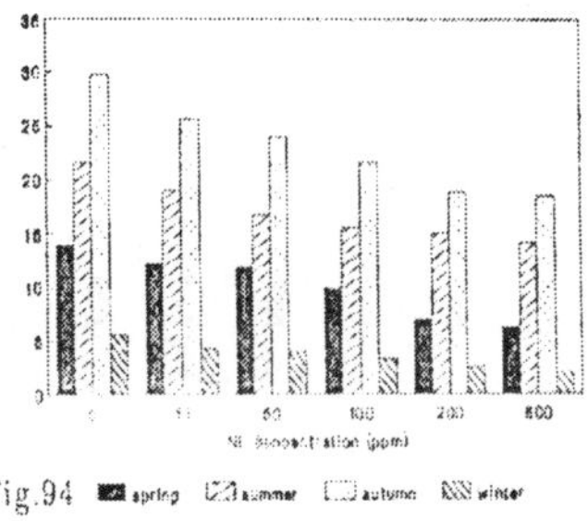

Fig.94

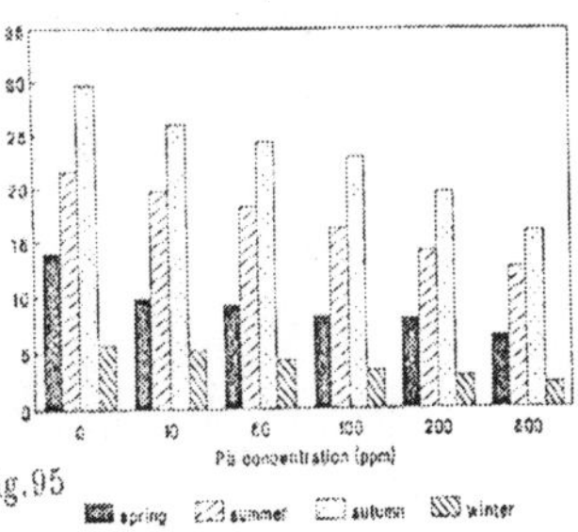

Fig.95

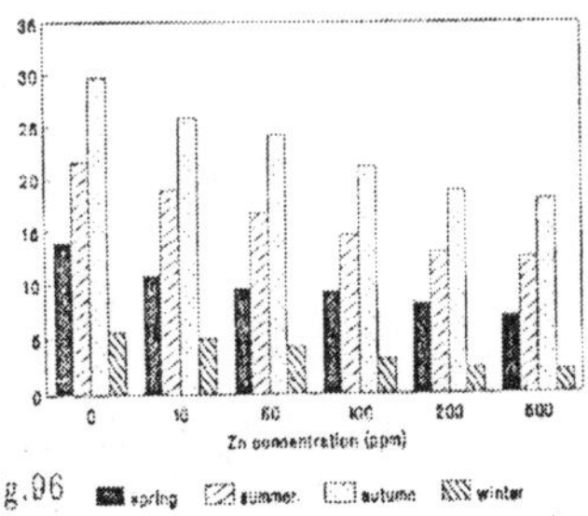

Fig.96

Fig.97–102 Phosphatase Activity on Non-mycorrhizal Root Surface

P-nitrophenol released mg/g dry wt/h

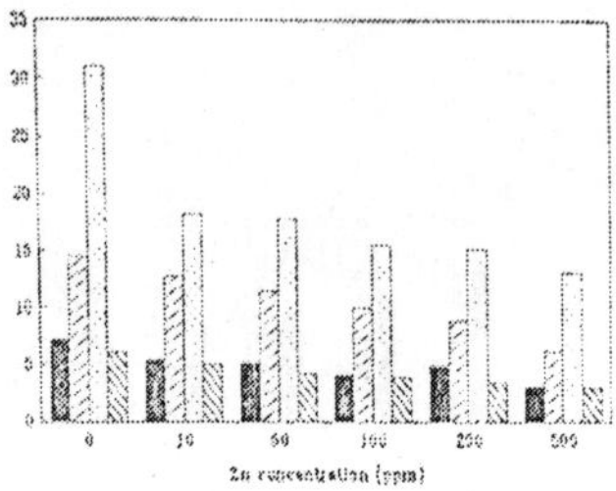

Fig.97 spring summer autumn winter

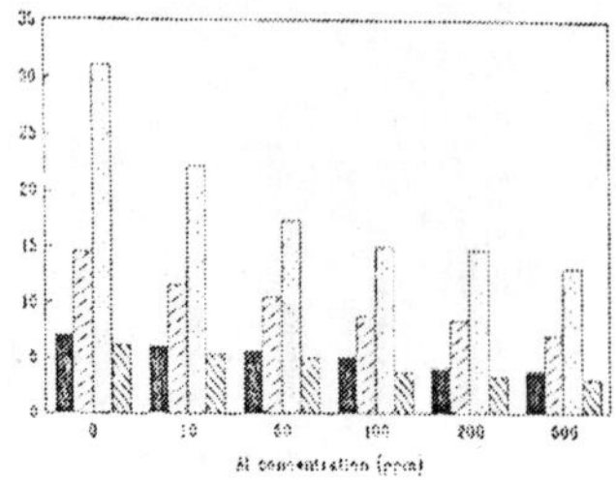

Fig.98 spring summer autumn winter

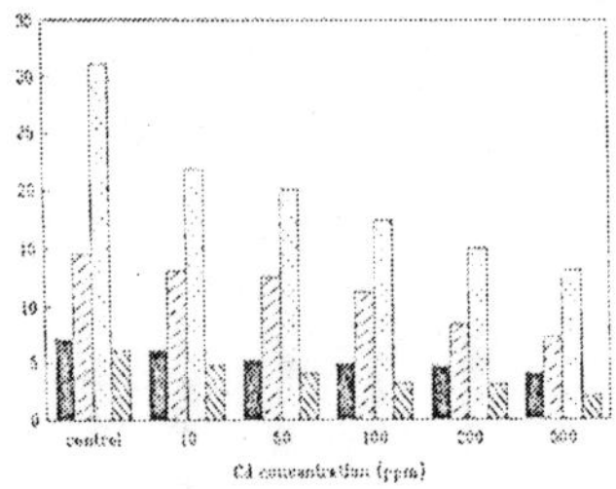

Fig.99 spring summer autumn winter

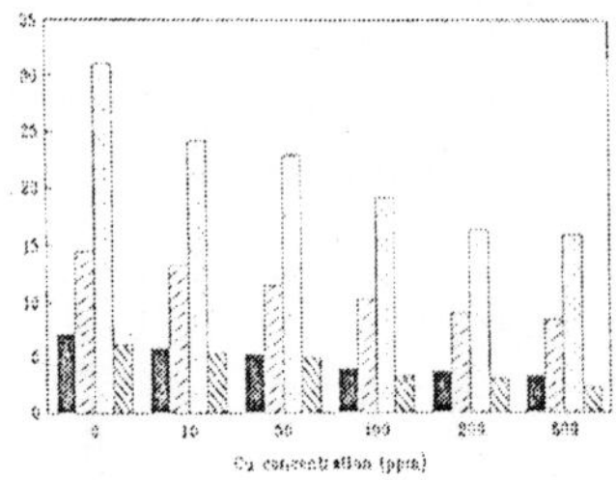

Fig.100 spring summer autumn winter

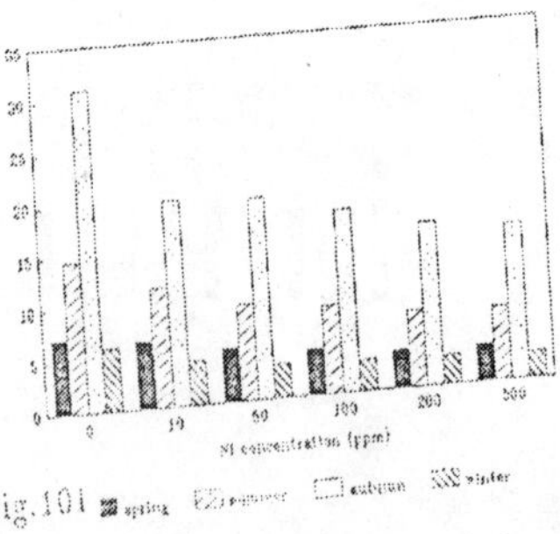

Fig.101 spring summer autumn winter

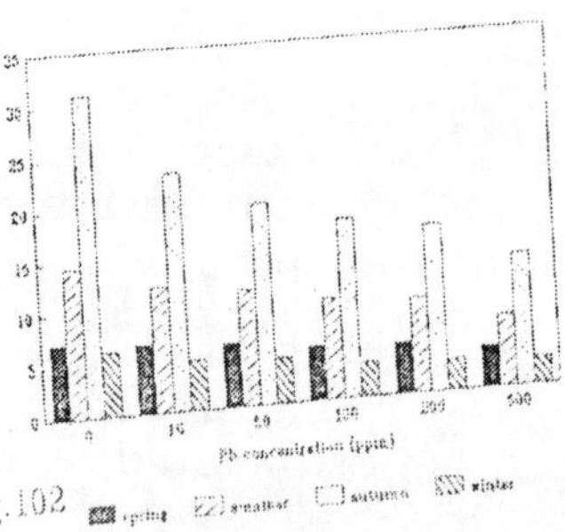

Fig.102 spring summer autumn winter

The increase dehydrogenase activity during the month of August may be the result of high microbial population numbers encountered in that month. The lower dehydrogenase activity in winter and spring was due to low microbial population numbers and the low carbon availability in addition to heavy metals pollution. Dormaar *et al.* (1984) demonstrated decrease in dehydrogenase activity in winter months due to water stress. Similarly, Tiwari *et al.* (1987) obtained significant correlation with microbial population numbers and soil moisture content.

There are reports of larger proportional decrease in dehydrogenase activity than in other indices of microbial activity in heavy metals contaminated soil. Dehydrogenase activity is considered to be caused by a broad group of endocellular enzyme (Skujins, 1978) which transfered electron and hydrogen from substrates to appropriate acceptors during initial stages of oxidation of organic compound. This concept of estimation of biological activity in soil by measuring dehydrogenase activity was first introduced by Lenhard (1956). Since then, this approach has been widely used.

Dehydrogenase activity was considerably decreased in the rhizospheric as well on the root surface with higher metal doses. Reddy and Faza (1989) also reported the decreased dehydrogenase activity in soil containing heavy metals. In case of rhizospheric soil highest percentage of inhibition was observed in *Scleroderma aurantium* inoculated seedlings with Pb, Cd and Ni. Dehydrogenase acticity in *Suillus luteus* inoculated rhizospheric soil and mycorrhizal roots showed almost the similar pattern at different metal treatments (Figs. 19-24 & 25-30). Maximum inhibition of activity was observed in Al treated soil and roots. The non-mycorrhizal roots and its rhizospheric soil showed high percentage of inhibition of dehydrogenase activity. Zn and Ni causes up to 50% inhibition in rhizospheric soil whereas in roots Cu and Pb had caused 44% inhibition in the enzyme activity.

The mixed mycobionts inoculated root surface and rhizospheric soil had more dehydrogenase activity than single mycobiont inoculation and non-mycorrhizal ones (Fig 31-36 & 37-42). The enhanced activity of enzyme in the root surface and in the rhizospheric soil was possibly due to presence of ectomycorrhizal fungi which enabled the seedlings to increase metabolic activities. Jha, (1992) correlated the high concentration of various enzymes like urease, dehydrogenase and phosphatase to the high microbial population in soil.

Heavy metals and urease activity:

Inoculation of ectomycorrhizal fungi harbored increased activity of urease enzyme. The urease activity was apparently less at high concentration (100 ppm and above) of Zn. Ni, Cu, Pb, Cd and Al treated seedlings. During spring to summer seasons, the urease activity remained almost constant but after September, the activity started to increase gradually and reached its peak in autumn. By contrast, in winter it decreased and remained constant throughout. The monthly fluctuations in urease activity was stronger than dehydrogenase and phosphatase. Seasonal fluctuations of enzyme activity appears to be dependent on factors, such as aeration, soil temperature and microflora (Burns, 1978). Metals like

Ni and Cd were found more toxic than rest of the metals. This could be due to their toxic nature when present in high amount. In case non-mycorrhizal roots, the percentage of inhibition was higher with an average of 45-50% in all the six different metals studied (Fig 43-48).

Study in field condition revealed that the urease activity was higher in seedlings infected with mixed inoculum compared to single inoculum in pots and the inhibition rate of enzyme by heavy metals was less both in rhizospheric soil as well as in root tissue (Fig 49-54, 55-60 & 61-66). The Cu treated root which was inoculated with mixed mycorrhizal fungi had minimum percentage of inhibition. The non-mycorrhizal seedlings however, exhibited highest percentage of inhibition especially in Cd, Ni and Pb treated soil (Fig 67-72).

The degree of inhibition in enzyme activity was dependent on the amount of metals added. Presence of low amount of organic matter was also an important factor for the intensity of inhibition. Soil organic matter is able to form complex metallic compound by cation exchange, absorption or chellation. The climatic and edaphic factors of soil may influence the microbial enzymes (Kiss *et al.*; 1975; Harrison, 1979) and exchange the quantity and quality of substrate in which they act. The increase enzyme activity was significantly correlated with organic C and total nitrogen (Frankenberger and Dick, 1983). High activity in ectomycorrhizal roots may be attributed to a faster rate of turnover of the organic matter. The high inhibition rate of urease activity in non-mycorrhizal root region due to heavy metal treatment may also be the result of low microbial numbers.

Heavy metals and phosphatase activity

Like the other two enzymes, phosphatase too showed significant seasonal variation Fig 73-78). Two periods of phosphatase activity were distinguishable , one with a higher activity in summer and another with a markedly low activity in winter. During summer months, its activity remained constant and increased slightly in September and reached the peak activity in autumn, but again in November it decreased and remained constant during winter. Harrison (1979) also obtained seasonal variation in phosphatase activity in polluted soil. The low phosphatase activity during winter may be due to low microbial population numbers, which lead to decreases mineralization and thus slowing the sucessional process. The highest percentage of inhibition in enzyme activity (50%) was observed in *S. aurantium* inoculated with Pb seedlings (Fig 79-84). The lowest rate of inhibition was observed in Cd and Cu treated seedlings (Fig 85-90 & 91-96). Non-mycorrhizal seedlings exhibited maximum inhibition in phosphatase acitivty (97-102), when exposed to heavy metals.

The enzyme activity was higher where seedlings were treated with mixed mycobionts in field condition. Possibly the presence of more than one ectomycorrhizal fungi enabled the seedlings to have their increased metabolic activities. Jha (1992) correlated the high concentrations of various enzymes like urease, dehydrogenase and phosphatase to high microbial population. The root growth was normally low in winter which leads to the assumption that along with high metals, low temperature added to the reduced microbial activity. The appreciable decrease in urease activity in rhizospheric soil receiving high metal concentration suggested that it is derived from living cells low quantity. Gianfreda *et al* (1994), reported that application of Cu in the form of fungicides altered the urease activity in soil.

A significant positive correlation was established between mycorrhizae infection and the activity of urease, phosphatase and dehydrogenase ($p<0.05$ and $p<0.01$ level) (table 4.1)

Table1. Correlation coefficient (r) values of mycorrhizal infection with enzyme activities of pine seedlings in pots (1) and in field (2) condition

		Mycorrhizal infection						
Enzymes		M1	M2	M3	M4	NM	MMF	MN
Phosphatase	1	0.91*	0.89*	0.88*	0.80**	NS	0.90**	NS
	2	0.92*	0.93*	0.96*	0.95*	NS	0.98*	NS
Dehydrogenase	1	0.87*	0.81**	0.91*	0.89*	NS	0.91*	NS
	2	0.96*	0.97*	0.91*	0.90*	NS	0.93*	NS
Urease	1	0.98*	0.91*	0.87*	0.80**	NS	0.92*	NS
	2	0.90*	0.94*	0.96*	0.86**	NS	0.90*	NS

M1= *C. graniforme*, M2= *S. leutus*, M3= *Boletus* sp, M4= *S. aurantium* NM= Non-mycorrhizal, MMF= Mixed mycorrhizal fungi

*= Significant at $p<0.01$ level, **= $p<0.05$ level

Significant variation was also found between the mycorrhizal and non-mycorrhizal ones ($p<0.01$) and between pots and field condition (table 4.2)

Table 2. Analysis of variance (F) values with the sampling periods, mycorrhizal and non-mycorrhizal and pots and fields with various parameters in pine seedlings

Sources of variance		Variation between sampling periods rrhizal	Variation between mycorrhizal and non-myco roots	Variation between pots and fields conditions
Phosphatase	1	13.32**	10.84**	12.31**
	2	7.3*	7.91*	5.58**
Urease	1	3.5**	7.9*	7.25*
	2	3.43**	3.13*	4.58**
Dehydrogenase	1	7.59*	6.33**	9.81**
	2	6.71*	6.28**	7.938

1= Root surface *=significant at p<0.01 level
2= Rhizospheric soil **=significant at p<0.05 level

The greater inhibition of enzymes in the presence of heavy metals could be due to inhibition of enzyme sites that were not available for catalysis. Stott *et al.* (1985) reported that metals like Cd, Cu, Ni, Pb and Zn may inhibit enzyme reaction by complexing the substrate or reaction with enzyme substrate complex. The mode of inhibition is dependent on the type of reaction or complexation produced. Tyler (1981) also observed that heavy metals inhibited a variety of mycorrhizal enzymes, indicating that the nature and type of inhibition varied among the metals used and the enzyme studied. However, little information is available on the inhibition of these enzymes on root surface and in rhizosphere soils by heavy metal ions. The degree of inhibition of urease, dehydrogenase and phosphatase activity on root surface and rhizosphere soil of pine seedlings by heavy metals was much smaller in mycorrhizal roots than non-mycorrhizal ones. Perhaps the binding of metal ions by fungal mycelium which consisted of fungal mantle and Hartig net could have taken place. This would explain why mycorrhizae in plants have lesser inhibition of growth by heavy metals compared to non-mycorrhizal ones. Denny and Wilkins (1987) also measured lower contents of Zn in the cortex of mycorrhizal roots than non-mycorrhizal birch plants.

All enzymes in soil are biologically significant as they are envolved in cycling of nutrients and can influence availability of nutrients elements to the plants. Microorganisms, rhizospheric region, active roots and dead cells all are considered the principal source of soil enzyme. Therefore, the non-mycorrhizal plants will have less access to the nutrients for their growth and developments, whereas mycorrhizal ones can sustain better growth due to availability of more nutrients generated in root region

References:

Antibus, R. K., Sinsabaugh, R. L. and Linkins, A. E. 1992. Phosphatase activities and phosphorus uptake from inositol phosphatase by ecomycorrhizal fungi. Can. J. Bot. 70:794-804.

Burns, R. G. 1978. Soil Enzymes. Academic Press. London.

Burns, R. G. 1982. Enzyme activity in soil: Location and possible role in microbial ecology. Soil Biol. Biochem. 14:423-427.

Denny, H. J. and Wilkins, D. A. 1987. Zn tolerance in *Betula* sp., variation in response to Zn among ectomycorrhizal associates. New Phytol. 106:535-544.

Dighton, J. and Jansen, S. E. 1990. Effect of air pollutants on ectomycorrhizas. Air Pollution Research Report. 30: ECC. Brussels.

Dodd, J. C., Burton, C. C., Burns, R. G and Jefferies, P. 1987.

Dormaar, J. F., Johnson, A. and smoliak, S. 1984. Seasonal changes in carbon content and dehydrogenase, phosphatase and urease activities in mixed Prairie and fescue grassland of horizon S. Journal of Range Management.. 37: 31-35.

Frankenberger, W. T. and Dick, W. A. 1983. Relationships between enzyme activities and microbial growth and activity indices in soil. Soil Science Society of American Journal. 47:945-951.

Gianfreda, L., Sannino, F., Ortega, N and Nannipieri, P. 1994. Activity of free and immobilized urease in soil: effects of pesticides. Soil Biol. Biochem. 26:777-784.

Harrison, A. F. 1979. Variation of four phosphorus properties in woodland soils. Soil Biol. Biochem. 11:393-403.

Jha, D. K., Sharma, G. D. and Mishra, R. R. 1992. Soil microbial population numbers and enzyme activities in relation to altitude and forest degradation. Soil Biol. Biochem. 24:761-768.

Kiss, S., Dragon-Bularda, M. and Radaleseu, D. 1975. Biological significance of soil enzyme accumulated in soil. Advances in Agronomy. 27: 25-87.

Lenhard, V. G. 1956. Die dehydrogenase aktivitat de Bodens als massfur die Mikroorganisms entatigkeit in Boden. Zeitschrift fur planzenernahrung Dungung Boden Kunde. 73:1-11.

Reddy, G.B. and Faza, A. 1989. Dehydrogenase activity in sludge amended soil. Soil Biol. Biochem. 21:327.

Rogers, H. T., Pearson, R. W. and Pierre, W. H. 1942. The source and phosphatase activity of exo-enzymes of corn and tomato roots. Soil Sci. 54:353-366.

Rousseau, J. V. D., Sylvia, D. M. and Fox, A. J. 1994. Contribution of ectomycorrhizae to the potential nutrient absorbing surface of pine. New Phytol. 129:638-644.

Skujins, J. 1978. History of abiotic enzyme research. In Soil enzymes (R. G. Burns Ed.) Academic Press. New York. pp. 1-49.

Spier, T. W., Lee, R., Pansier, E. A. and Cairns, A. 1980. A comparison of sulphatase, urease and protease activities in planted and fallow soils. Soil Biol. Biochem. 12:281-289.

Stott, D. E., Dick, W. A. and Tabatabai, M. A. 1985. Inhibition of pyrophosphatase activity in soil by trace elements. Soil Sci. B:112-117.

Tiwari, S. C., Tiwari, B. K. and Mishra, R. R. 1987. Temporal and depth-wise variations and dehydrogenase and urease activities and bacterial population in pineapple plantation soils. Proceedings of Indian National Science Academy. B53:173-176.

Tiwari, S. C., Tiwari, B. K. and Mishra, R. R. 1988. Enzyme activities in soil: Effect of leaching, ignition, autoclaving and fumigation. Soil Biol. Biochem. 20:(4) 583-585.

Tyler, A. E. S. and Alexander, I. 2005. The ectomycorrhizal symbiosis. Life in the real world. Mycologists. 19:201-112.

Heavy Metal Pollution and Mycorrhiza : **87-102**
Authors : Prof. G. D. Sharma and Dr. Tali Ajungla
Today & Tomorrow's Printers and Publishers. New Delhi-110 002

Chapter 5.

Microbes and Heavy metals in Environment

Ectomycorrhizae under heavy metal stress:

It has now been realized that the association of mycorrhizal fungi on trees naturally might well be manipulated to enhance the afforestation programmes. Artificial mass inoculation techniques have been developed to enable the use of selected ectomycorrhizal fungi either to seed or to colonize the plants at the seedlings stage. The response of mycorrhizal colonization among inoculated seedlings is greater under extreme conditions such as high temperature, metal contaminated soil and drought. Investigations have been done to understand the role of mycorrhizae in managing the different stress conditions. Various commercial inoculum formulations and inoculation techniques have been developed for the use in seedlings production systems (Marx and Bryan, 1975; Marx, 1975, 1980; Marx and Kenny, 1982; Marx and Cordell, 1989; Marx *et al.*,1991).

Certain plants can resist high concentration of heavy metals on soils. Much has been investigated recently on the apparent role of mycorrhizae for their ability to survive in metal contaminated soil. Mycorrhizal fungi bind metals and thus detoxify them. The acidity typical of most substrates of ectomycorrhizal plants, and in particular of the man-made substrates such as mine spoils which they colonize, is conducive to the solubilization of potentially toxic ions (Smith and Read, 1997). Amongst these, Al and Fe are most abundant in natural soil, while mine spoils are often polluted by Ni, Pb, Zn and Cd. These atmospheric input of heavy metals can lead to their accumulation in the soil of forest ecosystems especially of Pb and Cd (Zottl, 1985 and Kahle *et al.*, 1992). The survival of seedlings on metal contaminated sites determines its sensivity to metal toxicity. The colonizations of clonal cuttings of *Betula pubescens* by *Paxillus involutus* provides significant increase in resistant to Zn toxicity and the growth enhancement associated with mycorrhizae formation is related to reduced transfer to leaves (Brown and Wilkins, 1985; Denny and Wilkins, 1987). Similar result was obtained by Jones and Hutchinsons (1986), using Ni in seedlings of *B. papyrifera* which were colonized by *Scleroderma flavidum* , which is widely present on spoil heaps. Ni was concentrated in the roots of the plants where it appeared to be sequestered with polyphosphate (Jones and Hutchinsons, 1988). Higher concentrations of certain metals such as Cu, Pb and Zn act as environmental stress factors, as their toxic influence may bring about physiological reaction in the host plant (Levitt, 1980) resulting in reduction in vigor and growth, reproduction and in the extreme, even death. The translocation and accumulation of toxic metals may be concentrated in the tissues. This accumulation of various environmental pollutants in the plant surface is a contributing factor to the forest decline. During the last few years, the focus has been to study the toxicity of heavy metals on the plants due to increased industrial activity, excessive use of fertilizers and pesticides, and application of sewage and waste disposal on land and mining (Hutton and Symeon, 1986). Interaction between these contaminants in plants with respect to toxicity has been studied (Symenoides and Karataglis, 1992). However, information in the heavy metal toxicity to the mycorrhizal systems is still scarce.

Studies have revealed that ectomycorrhizal fungi accumulate heavy metals from highly diluted concentration in soils. The effectiveness in providing resistance to metal toxicity is dependant on ectomycorrhizal fungal species. In this vast changing environment, which is mainly created due to human activities, mycorrhizae still function on a global scale under natural condition. The impact of this atmospheric change upon mycorrhizal function and the role, if any, of mycorrhizas in determining ecosystem responses to the perturbation are subjects of great importance (Smith and Read, 1997) which are beginning to receive attention.

Mechanism of resistance:

Artificial inoculation of mycorrhizal fungi has been successfully introduced in many afforestation programmes. It has been suggested that ecomycorrhizae can ameliorate metal toxicity (Wilkins, 1991). Fungi in general are highly metal tolerant (Gadd, 1993). There are evidences that certain fungi can tolerate and protect the host plant against the toxicity caused by heavy metals. In *Picea abies*, tolerance of Cd was increased in seedlings inoculated with *Paxillus involutus* (Jentschke *et al.*, 1998). The mechanism by which mycorrhizal fungi ameliorate metal toxicity is by reducing metal uptake into critical location of the host plant as a result of adsorption of metals in fungal cell walls or intracellular sequestration in the mantle (Turnau *et al.*, 1993) and extrametrical mycelium (Denny and Wilkins, 1987; Colpaert and Van Assche, 1992, 1993; Marschner *et al.*, 1996). In recent studies, the presence of mycorrhizal symbiont appeared to reduce the metal toxicity. However, these symptoms persist in non-mycorrhizal seedlings. Seedlings roots were most susceptible to metal damage which became dark, short and thick. These results were similar to the findings of Mengel *et al.* (1982) who concluded that these symptoms were attributed to metal toxicity.

In Scanning Electron Microscopical studies (SEM), cellular and structural changes in roots of pine seedlings treated with heavy metals which appeared in both mycorrhizal and non-mycorrhizal roots could be due to breakdown of cytoplasmic structure, disruption of cell walls and cortical cells and accumulation of dense compound. The cytological changes appeared in metal-stress pine roots were similar to those that occurred in seedlings in which nutrient deficiency was. induced deliberately (Fink, 1991). It has been shown that in *Agrostis tenuis* the metal is confined to the roots, the main site of complexing being with cell wall (Wu *et al.*, 1975). At high levels of metals, however, inhibition of root extension and hence complexing ability occurred. In these circumstances the presence of an mycorrhizal fungal symbiont could be of considerable importance. The metal concentration in plant tissue was higher in non-mycorrhizal roots as compared to mycorrhizal roots. This suggested that production of dense fungal mycelium was an advantage for mycorrhizal host plant by reducing the uptake of heavy metals. However, once a saturation point was reached in the fungal mycelium, the translocation of metals to the host tissue also increased. In this circumstances, the rapid mycelial turnover which was associated with metal exclusion played a role in avoidance of toxicity. This hypothesis was also supported by Colpaert and Van Assche (1992).

Detailed information about responses to various mycorrhizal fungi to toxic metals is presented in a review by Hartley *et al.* (1997). The survival of long-lived trees on metalliferous soils may depend on mycorrhizae (Wilkinson and Dickinson, 1995). The fungal material can accumulate the heavy metals and act as a barrier for the toxic metals. In this way, mycorrhizae can help higher plants to adapt and to survive in contaminated habitats (Wilkinson and Dickinson, 1995). It is concluded that ectomycorrhizae had evolved resistance against heavy metals such as Zn, Cd, Ni, Cu, Pb and Al and that they play a role in metal resistance to plants. However, in metal contaminated soils the growth of mycorrhizal fungi can be inhibited. It is therefore important to consider the metal resistance not only to mycorrhizal symbiont but attributed also to its associated partners, since they have to survive during the life cycle alone, before the mycorrhizal association develops. It is very unlikely that the mycorrhizal fungi have direct influence on the transport of heavy metals in the plants. However, they could influence the amount of metal transported to the roots. This suggested that the extrametrical mycelia as well as mantle mycelia can complex a considerable amount of pollutants and thus strongly reduced the availability of the toxic ions in the soil.

Microorganisms in management of environmental pollution

The toxic heavy metals from industries, sewage sludge, factories, thermal power stations etc can be removed by physico-chemical means such as precipitation, electrolysis, ion-exchange and activated carbon exchange. Each of these have some disadvantages and advantages. On the other hand microbial biomass is also being used to remove heavy metals from waste. Microbes are being exploited to remove and recover heavy metals. The microbes are able to potentially degrade the pesticides used in plant protection, thus helping in maintaining the ecological balance. Substances, which are present in greater than natural abundance due to human activity, ultimately lead to detrimental effect on the environment as a whole in the form of a pollutant. Some examples are CO, SO_2 etc. In recent years, efforts are being made to control the increasing problem of environmental pollution.

Heavy metals such as Pb, Cd etc. are found in several modern industries and waste effluents. These metals have potential toxic effect on human being too. These effluents need to be treated and removed before being discharged to natural land and water. Several toxic heavy metals that are present in waste of thermal power stations, industries, sewage sludges etc are being treated to recover the metals through the activity of microorganisms. This microbial biomass has been used successfully for removal of heavy metals from the wastes. The metals are either adsorbed on the cell surface or simply entrapped in the bioflocs (Sreekrishnan and Tyagi, 1999). The ability of certain microorganisms to solubilize metals is an interesting biological phenomenon. It has now been realized that the liberal and indiscriminate use of metal due to industrialization and urbanization has resulted in much ecological panic to all living components of the earth. Certain heavy metals like Zn, Cd, Pb, Ni, Sb etc act as environmental stress factors due to their persistence in nature. Plants capable of accumulating high concentrations of metals such as zinc, nickel, cadmium, lead, copper and cobalt could provide an effective and practical method of cleaning–up heavily polluted soils (Dubey and Maheshwari, 2009). There are opportunities to remove the heavy metal pollutants in the environment using the metal tolerant plants.

There are evidences that microbes such as fungi, bacteria, algae etc have the capability to tolerate heavy metals. Bacteria like *Thiobacillus ferroxidant, Thiobacillus thiooxidant, Streptococcus agalactiae, Pseudomonas aeruginosa, Staphylococcus aureus* etc. have been long considered as important bacteria which directly attacked on metal sulfides. These bacteria resistant to heavy metals were frequently isolated from soil and water. Bacteria like *T. ferroxidants, T. thioparus* or *T. thiooxidants* are used for removal of heavy metals from sewage sludges through bioleaching process (Sreekrishnan and Tyagi, 1999). Plasmids have also been reported to be responsible for heavy metal tolerance in bacteria. Recombinant bacteria have also been investigated recently for removal of heavy metals from contaminated water.

A good number of fungi exhibit the tolerance to heavy metal toxicity. Species of *Streptomyces* showed great ability to absorb heavy metals such as Zn, Pb, Mg etc. The biomass of *Rhizopus arrhizus* can accumulate up to 180mg/g dry wt. of uranium and thorium. Likewise *Saccharomyces cerevisaiae* can accumulate uranium from metal solution and *Penicilium chrysogenum* for radium removal (Sharma, 1988). It has been reported that fungi tend to survive heavy metal stress either by adaptation or mutation. Studies have revealed that the lead and copper were accumulated by fungi among the heavy metals. Dubey and Dwivedi (1985) reported that *Macrophomina phaseolina* has shown tolerance up to 500 ppm of cadmium *in vitro.* However, the toxicity of this metal was influenced by pH, zinc and manganese in the medium. The microbes will extract the heavy metals and sequester them inside their cell membranes.

Several species of algae have been reported to tolerate heavy metal contaminants. The green alga such as *Chlorella,* blue green algae such as *Anabaena* and marine algae and macrophytes have also been used for removal of heavy metals from aquatic habitats. At present, several biotechnological approaches have been recommended where metal extracting microbes such as algae can be grown in ponds rich in heavy metals due to discharges from factory effluents.

Earlier the removal and cleaning of heavy metals pollution were mainly through the physical and chemical methods. Certain techniques such as oxidation, reduction, precipitation, ultrafiltration etc. were used. In recent years, however, use of microorganisms to remove heavy metals contaminants is an alternative to physical and chemical methods. Certain microorganisms that can absorb heavy metal have been shown (table 5.1).

Table 5.1: Microorganisms involved in metal removal from industrial wastewater (based on Bitton, 1999).

Microorganisms	Metals removed
Aspergillus niger	Copper, cadmium, zinc
A. oryzae	Cadmium
Chlorella vulgaris	Gold, copper, mercury, zinc
Penicilium spinulosum	Copper, cadmium, zinc
Rhizopus arrhizus	Uranium
Saccharomyces cerevisiae	Uranium
Trichoderma viride	Copper
ATM-Bioclaim™	Biotechnology-based use of granulated product derived from biomass.

There are four different types of mechanisms by which microorganisms operate in removal of heavy metals from the metal polluted environment. These are viz. **adsorption**: where the microbes cell surfaces that are negatively charged are able to bind to the metal ions. **Complexation**: chellation of metal ions occurs, certain organic acids such as citric acid, lactic acid, malic acid etc. are produced by microorganisms. It is believed that metal ions can bound to wall polymers at the cell wall, such as chitin or melanin and inside the cells they might be rendered harmless to complexation and compartmentation. **Precipitation:** Bacteria like *Desulfovibrio* and *Desulfotomaculum* can transform SO_4 to H_2S which promote extracellular precipitation of insoluble metal sulfides. Some other types of bacteria that produce ammonia which precipitate the metals as sulfides or hydroxides. **Volatilization:** Methylation of Hg^{2+} and conversion to dimethyl mercury which is a volatile compound takes place through the activity of some bacteria.

Bioremediation

At present, bioremediation is considered as most efficient alternate technology to reduce environmental pollution, restoring the contaminated sites and to prevent further pollution in the environment. The use of living organisms, mostly microorganisms to reduce and prevent environmental pollutants through waste treatment is known as **bioremediation**. This environmental friendly technology is presently given a top priority to clean up environmental pollution. The treatment of effluents through biological means has long been practicing in many places, but some constituents of these effluents are unable to clean through conventional methods of treatment. Bioremediation of pollutants has overcome this problem.

Role of microbes in bioremediation

Environmental biotechnology has great potential in monitoring environmental pollution, restoration of environmental quality, generation of various organic chemicals from microbial biomass etc. using biotechnological methods, new types of specific proteins, peptides and biomimetic adsorbers have been developed for controlling the pollutants. Many new microbial based technologies are being developed to degrade environmental pollutants. The use of living organisms for treatment of municipal and industrial wastes mainly to control pollution has been expanding worldwide. Many researches have been undertaken to employ microorganisms for bioremediation. There is search for naturally occurring microbes that have better pollutant degradation kinetics, attack a wider range of heavy metals for the microbial growth conditions (Sharma, 1998). There is also need for microbes that can tolerate extremes of environmental conditions such as alkalinity, high temperature etc. which becomes unfavorable for growth of most of the microorganisms. The microbes are known to extract heavy metals and sequester them inside the cell-membranes.

Investigations are on to develop new microbial strains with potential for biodegradation. This kind of genetically modified microbes can be used to degrade those pollutants which is otherwise not possible through the naturally occurring microorganisms.

Microorganisms can acclimatize themselves to toxic waste materials and naturally new resistant genes developed. Such strains are selected and can be used for microbial environmental clean-up approaches.

Now microorganisms are being discovered which can breakdown the plastic shells of duroplastics. Microbes such as fungi and bacteria have been used to clean up oil contaminated water reservoirs and water supplies. Bacterial and algal species are used to extract metals from the industrial effluents. Biotechnological approaches are recommended, where metal extracting algae can be grown in ponds to extract heavy metals. Fungi like *Rhizopus arrhizus* have been demonstrated to trap the metallic cations solution. This may be due to their peculiarity in cell composition, thus being ecologically sound.

A strain of *Pseudomonas aeruginosa* has the potential to emulsify oil in water and thus facilitate to remove oil spills. This *P. aeruginosa* can also accumulate uranium. The biorecovery systems company patented a product called Algasorb for absorbing heavy metals ions from ground water and wastewater (Dara, 2002). Dead algae is being trapped using silica gel to prepare algasorb. Trapping of algal cells is mainly to protect the cells from other destructive microorganisms. Using the algasorb, heavy metal ions can be stripped out easily. Some bacteria such as *Thiobacillus* and *Pseudomonas aerugenosa* have potential to accumulate heavy metals such as silver and uranium.

The sewage of modern industries contains heavy metals like mercury, lead and cadmium which causes poisoning. Metals like mercury is known to cause food poisoning that attack nervous system of the patients. Lead causes mental retardation of the children. The factory effluents contain lead which needs to be treated before being discharged to the environment. The toxic effluents from the industries have been treated with chemical and physical means. But in recent years, biotechnological approaches, involving biodegradation and bioremediation have become popular.

Application of bioremediation:

The use of living organisms to clean up waste materials is practiced worldwide. This technology of using microorganisms to clean the environment is much needed because certain chemicals and wastes accumulate in soils and water which threaten the environment quality. Many research projects are being carried out in search for naturally occurring microorganisms that have better pollutant degradation potential and also could attack a wider range of pollutants. The category of microbes which can tolerate extremes of different environmental conditions such as high temperature, alkalinity etc. are needed to widen the scope of bioremediation. Recently, through genetic engineering new strains of microbes have been developed that have better biodegradative quality. The modified microbes may be produced through the genetic coding for attack of complex chlorinated hydrocarbons such as dioxins which are non-degradable by naturally occurring microbes (Sharma, 1998). Through this emerging new technology, many microbes will be able to survive and grow in the harsh environment. A research team in Japan has isolated a species of *Pseudomonas* that can grow in solvents containing 50% toluene, a condition that kills most microorganisms through disruption of cell membranes. By adding appropriate genes for catabolic enzymes, many microbes can breakdown the toxic chemicals through bioconversions.

Bioremediation can be used to treat heavy metal contaminated sites. Many microorganisms, such as algae, bacteria, fungi as well as higher plants are able to remove these pollutants from the environment.

References:

Ashida, J., Higashi, N. and Kikuchi, Y. 1975. Protoplasma. 57:27-32.

Bitton, G. 1994. Wastewater Microbiology. Wilet-Liss, Gainsville. 210, 76.

Brown, M. T. and Wilkins, D. A. 1985. Zn tolerance in mycorrhizal *Betula*. New Phytol. 99:101-106.

Colpaert, J. V. and Van Assche, J. A. 1992. Zinc toxicity in ectomycorrhizal *Pinus sylvestres*. Plant Soil. 143:201-211.

Colpaert, J. V. and Van Assche, J. A. 1993. The effects of cadmium on ectomycorrhizal *Pinus sylvestries*. New Phytol. 123:325-333.

Dara, S. S. 2002. Biotechnology and its application in environmental pollution. In: Environmental Chemistry and Pollution Control. 217-224.

Denny, H. J. and Wilkins, D. A. 1987. Zinc tolerance in *Betula* spp.1. Effect of external concentrations of zinc on growth and uptake. New Phytol. 106:517-524.

Denny, H. J. and Wilkins, D. A. 1987. Zn tolerance in *Betula* spp. IV. The mechanism of ectomycorrhizal amelioration of zinc toxicity. New Phytol. 106:545-553.

Dubey, R. C. and Dwivedi, R. S. 1985. Proc. Ind. Natl. Sci. Acad. B51:259-264.

Dubey, R. C and Maheshwari, D. K. 2009: Microbiology. Environmental Biology. 814-852.

Fink, S. 1991. Structural changes in conifer needle due to Mg and K deficiency. Fert. Res. 27:23-27.

Hartley, J., Cairney, J.W.G., Meharg, A. A. 1997. Do ectomycorrhizal fungi exhibit adaptive tolerance to potentially toxic metals in environment. Plant Soil. 189:303-319.

Hutton, M. and Symeon, C. 1986. The quantities of cadmium, lead, mercury and arsenic entering the U. K environment from human activities. Sci. Total Environ.57:129-150.

Jentschke, G., Winter, S and Godbold, D. L. 1998. Ectomycorrhizae and cadmium toxicity in Norway spruce seedlings. Tree Physiol. 18:

Jones, M. D. and Hutchinsons, T. C. 1986. the effects of mycorrrhizal infections on the response of *Betula papyrifera* to Ni and Cu. New Phytol. 102:429-442.

Jones, M. D. and Hutchinsons, T. C. 1988. Nickel toxicity in mycorrhizal birch seedlings infected with *Lactarius rafus* or *Scleroderma flavadum*. Effect on growth, photosynthesis, respiration and transpiration. New Phytol. 108:451-459.

Kahle, H. and Breckle, S. W. 1992. Blieund cadmium- Zietbombe in unseren waldboden. Biologie in Unserer Ziet. 22:21-27.

Levitt, J. 1980. Response of plants to environmental stresses second Edn., Academic Press, New York.

Marshner, P., Godbold, D. L. and Jentschke, G. 1996. Dynamics of lead in mycorrhizal and non-mycorrhizal Norway spruce (*Picea abies* L Karst). Plant Soil. 178:239-240.

Marx, D. H. and Bryan, W. C. 1975. Growth and ectomycorrhizae development of loblolly pine seedlings in fumigated soil infected with fungal symbiont. *Pisolithus tinctorius*. Forest Science. 21:245-254.

Marx, D. H. 1975. Mycorrhizae and establishment of trees on striped-mined land. Ohio Journal of Science. 75:288-297.

Marx, D.H. 1980. Role of mycorrhizae in forestation of surface-mines. On: Proceedings of symposium on trees for reclamation interstate mining. Compact Commission and USDA forest Service. Lexington, Kentucky, USA, 109:116.

Marx, D. H. and Kenny, D. S. 1982. Production of ectomycorrhizal fungus inoculum In: Methods and Principles of mycorrhizal research (Ed. N. C Schenck). American Phytopathological Society. St. Paul Minnesota, USA. 131-146.

Marx, D. H. and Cordell, C. E. 1989. The use of specific mycorrhizas to improve artificial forestation practices In: Biotechnology of fungi for improving plant growth (Ed. J. M. Whipps and R. D. Lumsden). British Mycological Society. Cambridge University Press. Cambridge, U. K. 1-25.

Marx, D. H., Ruehle, J. L. and Cordell, C. E. 1991. Methods for studying nursery and field response of trees to specific ectomycorrhizae. Methods in Microbiology. 23:383-411.

Mengel, K. and Kirby, E. A. 1982. Principles of plant nutrition, 3rd Edn. Bund, A. G. Bern

Sharma, P. D. 1998. An emerging biotechnology using microorganism for environmental clean-up. In: Microbiology and Plant Pathology. 294-213.

Sharma, P. D. 1998. Environmental Microbiology. Environmental Quality: Biodegradation of waste and Pollutants (Microbiology of sewage and petroleum). In: Microbiology and Plant Pathology. 281-293.

Smith, S. E. and Read, D. J. 1997. mycorrhizas in managed environments: forest production, interaction with other microorganisms and pollutants. In; Mycorrhizal symbiosis. Academic Press. London. 470-487.

Sreekrishnan, T. R. and Tyagi, R. D. 1999. Metal removal from sewage sludge: Bioengineering and biotechnological applications. In: heavy metal stress in plants, from molecules to ecosystems. (eds. M.N.V. Prasad and J. Hagemeyer). 331-348.

Symenoides, L. and Karataglis, S. 1992. Interactive effects of Cd, Pb and Zn on root growth of two metal tolerant genotypes of *Holcus lanatus* L. Biometals. 5:173-178.

Tarnau, K., Kottke, Oberwinkle and F. I. 1993. *Paxillus involutus, Pinus sylvestries* mycorrhizae from heavy metal polluted forest. 1. Element localization using electron energy loss spectroscopy and imaging. Bot. Acta. 106:213-219.

Wu, L. and Antonovis, J. 1975. Zn and Cu uptake by *Agrostis stolonifera* tolerant to both Zn and Cu. New Phytol. 75:231-237.

Wilkins, D. A. 1991. Der Einflub von cadmium auf das waschstum von Fischter am Beipiel der mykorrhizapilze *Laccaria laccata* and *Paxillus involutus.* M. Sc. Thesis. University of Gottingen.

Wilkinson, D. M. and Dickinson, N. M. 1995. Metal resistance in trees: the role of mycorrhizae. Oikos. 72:298-300.

Zottl, H. W. 1985. Heavy metals levels and cycling in forest ecosystems. Experentia. 41:1104-1113.

Heavy Metal Pollution and Mycorrhiza : **103-122**
Authors : Prof. G. D. Sharma and Dr. Tali Ajungla
Today & Tomorrow's Printers and Publishers. New Delhi-110 002

Chapter 6

Mechanism of Heavy Metal Tolerance in Plants

Introduction

Heavy metals are among the most toxic inorganic substances which have contaminated large area of land due to use of sludge, pesticides, fertilizers, and emissions from municipal waste incinerators, car exhausts, residues from metalliferous mines, and smelting industries. Plants present a dilemma that metal ions such as copper (Cu), zinc (Zn) , iron (Fe), manganese (Mn) and nickel (Ni), etc., are trace nutrients taking part in redox reactions, electron transfers, a multitude of enzyme catalyzed reactions, and structural functions in nucleic acid metabolism, while these same heavy metals, and the even more potent ions of Cd, Hg, Pb, Ag, As, Al, etc. are strongly poisonous to metalsensitive enzymes, resulting in growth inhibition and death of the organism. How do plants regulate their metabolism in response to heavy metals and protect themselves against metal poisoning? The answer lies in understanding the mechanism of detoxification and tolerance of plants to heavy metal stress.

Metal toxicity and tolerance in plants is a subject that has been broadly reviewed (Hall, 2002; Clemens *et aL*, 2002; Benavides *et al.*, 2005,Misra and Dubey, 2006; Panda, 2008, Pal and Rai, 2009). The presence of both essential and non essential heavy metals in the atmosphere, soil and water, in excessive amounts, can cause serious problems to all organisms. Knowledge of metal-plant interactions is important for the safety of the environment, but also for reducing the risks associated with the introduction of trace metals into the food chain. Heavy metals are also included in the main category of environmental pollutants as they can remain in the environment for long periods; their accumulation is potentially hazardous to humans, animals and plants (Benavides *et al.*, 2005; Gratão *et al.*, 2005; Panda, 2008). We have witnessed in the last few decades a dramatic increase in contamination of the environment, including soil, air and water. It is well known that any pollutant, heavy metals in particular, has the potential to cause damage to plants, which, in turn, respond to the stress to survive. Heavy metal-induced oxidative stress in plants disturbing the balance between oxidants and antioxidants in the cell. The sensitivity of plants to heavy metals depends on an interrelated network of physiological and molecular mechanisms that includes uptake and accumulation of metals through binding to extracellular exudates and cell wall, complexation of ions inside the cell by various substances, for example, organic acids, amino acids, feffitins, phytochelatins, and metallothioneins ; general biochemical stress defense responses such as the induction of antioxidative enzymes and activation or modification of plant metabolism to allow adequate functioning of metabolic pathways and rapid repair of damaged cell structures (Hall, 2002; Shankar *et al.*,

2005; Azevado and Azevedo, 2006, Tiwari *et al.*, 2006; Panda *et al.*, 2008). The present review is an insight into the mechanisms of heavy metal detoxification ·in plants.

Biochemical mechanism of heavy metal detoxification in plants

Reactive oxygen species (ROS) such as O_2^-, H_2O_2, and ^-OH are commonly generated under stress conditions and bear strong oxidizing activities that can attack all types of biomolecules. In fact, these oxygen species represent intermediates emerging during the successive reduction of O_2^- to H_2O_2 (Sharma *et al.*, 2008). Plants exposure to certain heavy metal ions shifts the balance of free radical metabolism towards an accumulation of H_2O_2. In the presence of redox active transition metals such as Cu and Fe^2, H_2O_2 can be converted to the highly reactive ^-OH molecule in a metal-catalyzed reaction via the Fenton reaction. The oxidized metal ions undergo a re-reduction in a subsequent reaction with superoxide radicals (O_2^-). An alternative mechanism of ^-OH formation directly from H_2O_2 and O_2^-, is the metal-independent Haber Weiss reaction

Fenton reaction;

H_2O_2 + Fe^{2+} /Cu^+ '‡$^\cdot OH$ + OH^- + Fe^{3+} /Cu^{2+}

$^\cdot O_2^-$ + Fe^3 /Cu^{2+} '‡Fe^2 /Cu $^+$ O_2

Haber Weiss reaction;

H_2O_2+ $^\bullet O_2^\bullet$ '‡$^\cdot OH$ + OH^- + O_2

The $^\cdot OH$ molecule is one of the most reactive species known. Because of its ability to initiate radical chain reactions it is very likely responsible for irreversible chemical modifications of various cellular components. Another ROS that might be involved mainly in lipid peroxidation is the protonated form of $^{\cdot}O_2^-$, the hydroperoxyl radical ($^{\cdot}O_2^-$ H). These species exist in equilibrium. Possibly metal ions inhibit the activities of antioxidative enzymes especially of glutathione reductase, and also raise a transient depletion of GSH (Xiang and Olliver, 1998; Zhang *et al.*, 2008). Thus, a natural accumulation of ROS would be the consequence. Heavy metals like Cu, Zn, Cd, Cr, Pb, Hg, As, Fe...etc under toxic concentration inactivates enzymic antioxidant defense system in plants resulting into increased ROS signaling generally leading to death of a plants (Panda and Patra, 1997; Sanita di Toppi *et al.*, 2002; Panda *et al.*, 2003; Panda and Choudhury, 2005)

In response to toxic levels of heavy metals, plants synthesize Cys-rich, metal-binding peptides including phytochelatins, metallothioneins and organic acids. Therefore, heavy metals can be detoxified by chelation and sequestration in the vacuole (Clemens, 2001; Cobbett and Goldsbrough, 2002), and various membrane transport systems play an important role in metal ion homeostasis and tolerance (Hall and Williams, 2003) (Fig. 1). Heavy metal (Cu, Zn ...etc.) ions play essential roles in many physiological processes. In trace amounts, several of these ions are required for metabolism, growth, and development. However, problems arise when cells are confronted with an excess of these vital ions or with non-nutritional ions that lead to cellular damage (Bazaz *et al.*, 1992; Kim *et al.*, 2003; Tiwari *et al* ., 2006; Panda ,2007; Nada *et al.*, 2007; Wang *et al.*, 2008). Heavy metal toxicity comprises inactivation of biomolecules by either blocking essential functional groups or by displacement of essential metal ions (Goyer, 1997). Understanding how plants accumulate and store metal ions is relevant to two important applications: metal nutrition – for humans and in agriculture; and metal detoxification – using plants as biological detoxification systems for the 'phytoremediation' of metal contamination in the environment. Knowing how plant regulate essential metal ion metabolism will contribute to improvements in essential metal ion nutrition of plant and utilizing them as potential source of phytoremediation. Similarly, knowledge of the mechanisms by which metals, both essential and nonessential, can be sequestered, stored and detoxified in various organisms may contribute to the optimisation of phytoremediation processes (Clemens *et al.*, 2002). It has been well studied that some biochemical compounds involved in the physiological mechanisms of plants exposed to heavy metals are proteins capable of making linkages with metals, thereby forming complex biochemical compounds called metal-proteins, metallothionein and peptides like phytochelatins. Besides these, organic acids and amino acids takes active part in detoxification of heavy metals in plants (Hall, 2002; Mishra and Dubey, 2006; Pal and Rai, 2009).

Extracellular Mechanism

A general mechanism for detoxification of heavy metals in plants is the distribution of metals to apoplast tissues like trichone and cell walls, and chelation of the metals by a ligand, followed by the sequestration of the metal–ligand complex into the vacuole. Cell walls may play an important role in detoxifying metals in plant cells of the Ni and Zn/Cd hyperaccumulating plant species. About 60–70% of Ni and/or Zn accumulated is distributed in the apoplast cell walls. However, molecular bases of metal detoxification by cell walls are not well understood. At extracellular level plants protect itself from metals poisoning either by immobilizing them with their root exudates or some mycorrihzal association takes part in metal detoxification (Hall, 2002; Ajungla and Sharma, 2003; Mishra and Dubey, 2006). In many plant species, Cd can be immobilized by cell wall and extracellular carbohydrates (Mishra and Dubey, 2006), Cd ions mostly seem to bind pectic sites and histidyl groups of the cell wall. Possible involvement of histidine and citrate has been suggested in root exudates that reduces Ni-uptake and helps in Ni-detoxification (Salt *et al.,* 2000). In cereals also better tolerance to Al toxicity is associated with root exudation of citric acid, malic acid, succinic acid, oxalic acid and other organic acids (Bertrand and Guary, 2002). Activation of organic acid efflux occurs rapidly without any measurable delay after exposure to Al in several plant species (Ryan *et al.,* 2001). Efflux of citrate and malate from plant roots in response to Al occurs by activation of anion-channels located in the plasma membrane (Ryan *et al.,* 2001). There are accumulating evidences in support of mycorrhizal involvement in host plant metal detoxification more specially the ectomycorrhizal association (Hall, 2002). The fungi employ the same strategy for metal detoxification as adopted by higher plants i.e., binding to extracellular materials or sequestration in the vacuolar compartment (Hall, 2002). Ectomycorrbizas restrict metal movement to host roots by exclusion processes (Jentschke and Godbold, 2000). Some mycorrhization stimulales the phenolic defense system in mycorrhizal symbiosis (Schlltzendubel and Polle, 2002). Cellular mechanisms proposed to be involved in metal uptake, sequestration and its detoxification in plants have been outlined in Fig. 1.

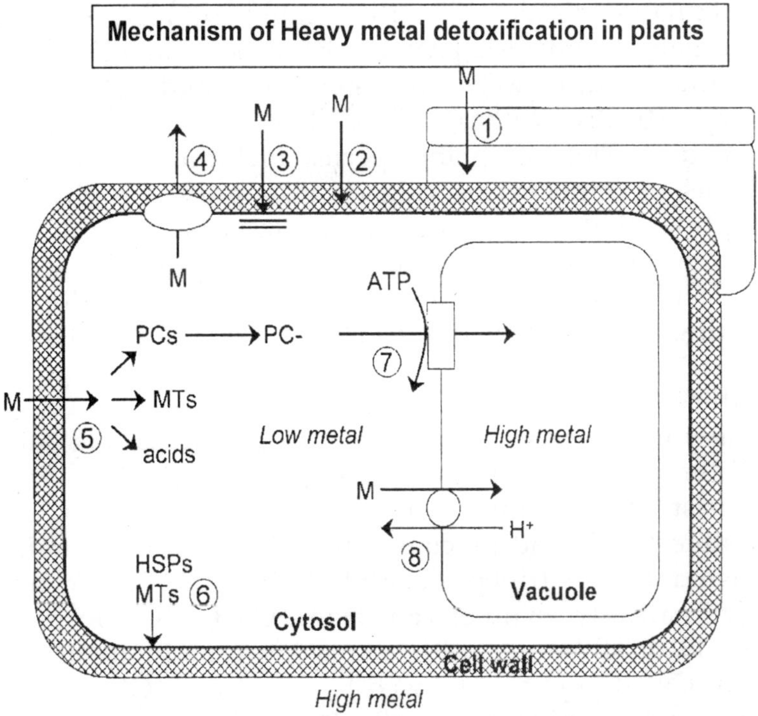

Fig. 1 Cellular mechanism of metal detoxification and tolerance in higher plants

1. Metal movement to roots. 2. Binding to Cell wall and Root exudates.3. Reduced influx across plasma membrane 4. Active efflux into apoplast. 5. Chelation in cytosol by various ligands 6. Repair and protection of plasma membrane under stress conditions. 7. Transport of PC-Cd complex into the vacuole. 8.Transport and accumulation of metals in vacuole (Modified from **Hall, 2002**)

Intracellular metal detoxification in plants

Intracellular complexation involves peptide ligands, such as metallothioneins (MTs) and PCs. MTs are cystein-rich polypeptides, first identified in mammalian tissues as Cd-binding peptides . Several MT genes, and also proteins have been identified in plants. While MTs are gene-encoded, PCs are enzymatically synthesized. PCs have been identified in a wide variety of plant species including monocots, dicots, gymnosperms, algae. PCs are a family of peptides that were first identified in yeast. Most of the current knowledge of these peptides has resulted from molecular-genetic studies on yeast and Arabidopsis during the last few years (Yung *et al.,* 2005; Mishra and Dubey, 2006; Pal and Rai, 2009). PCs are rapidly induced in cells and tissues exposed to a range of heavy metal ions, such as Cd, Ni, Cu, Zn, Ag, Hg, and Pb, and anions, such as arsenate and selenite . PCs consist of only three amino acids, glutamine (Glu), cystine (Cys), and glycine (Gly). They are structurally related to the tripeptide glutathione (GSH), and are enzymatically synthesized from GSH. PCs form a family of structures with increasing repetitions of the -Glu-Cys dipeptide followed by a terminal Gly, (-Glu-Cys)n-Gly, where n is generally in the range of 2–5, but can be as high as 11 . It was shown that GSH-deficient mutants of Arabidopsis are also PC deficient and Cd sensitive . GSH-dependent PC synthase activity was identified in cultured cells of *Silene cucubalis* . The enzyme is active only in the presence of metal ions, such as Cd, Cu, Zn, Ag, Hg, and Pb. Similar activities have been identified in *Arabidopsis* , tomato , and pea . Several studies have suggested that PC synthase activity is regulated at the level of enzyme activation by metal ions. The fact that PC synthase activity has an important role in Cd tolerance was shown in *Vigna angularis* (Azuki beans) that are hypersensitive to Cd. Cell-suspension cultures of Azuki bean did not synthesize PCs when challenged with Cd. These cells also lacked PC synthase activity. Externally applied GSH failed to stimulate PC synthesis or confer Cd tolerance to the cells, which demonstrated the importance of PC synthesis in Cd/metal tolerance in plants.

Phytochelatins and Metallothioneins

Phytochelatins (PCs) were first discovered as Cd-binding "Cysteins A and B" in a fission yeast and then in many plants as the major components of Cd-binding complexes. Phytochelatins (PCs) are enzymatically synthesized peptides known to involve in heavy metal detoxification and accumulation, which have been measured in plants grown at high heavy metal concentrations, but few studies have examined the response of plants even at lower environmentally relevant metal concentrations. Recently, genes encoding the enzyme PC synthase have been identified in plants and other species enabling molecular biological studies to untangle the mechanisms underlying PC synthesis and its regulation. Several published literature revealed advances in structure of PCs, their biosynthetic regulation, roles in heavy metal detoxification and/or accumulation, and PC synthase gene expression for better understanding of mechanism involved in detoxification of heavy metals in plants (Mishra and Dubey, 2006; Pal and Rai, 2009).

PCs have the general structure of (gð-glutamyl-cysteinyl)n-glycine (n=2-ll) and the variants with the repeated gð-glutamyl-cysteinyl units are formed in some plants and yeast They are capable of binding to various metals including Cd, Cu, Zn or As via the sulfhydryl and carhoxyl residues, but their biosyntheses are controlled preferentially by the metal. PCs are synthesized from glutathione (gð-g1utaml-cysteinyl-glycine) in steps mediated by PC synthase. Inhibition studies of PC biosynthesis via glutathione have demonstrated their fundamental roles in the metal detoxification in yeast and fungi, green algae and some aquatic plants, and also in the suspension-cultured cells and intact tissues in higher plants. Over-expression of PC synthase genes increases the metal tolerance in yeast and bacteria efficiently but not always in higher plant tissues especially in metal-accumulating species. "Hyperaccumulators" of Cd, Zn, Ni or As in terrestrial plants have a common features where massive metal transport to shoots prevails, besides the ability of their roots to form PCs. Hence PC based metal detoxification might be the primary defense mechanism established in lower plants and the additional PC-independent mechanism via vascular transport system became established later in higher plants. Existence of the PC-dependent and independent mechanisms at the metal-binding sites in the symplast and apoplast of shoots might improve metal detoxification and the tolerance characteristics of higher plants under heavy metal stress.

Metallothioneins (MTs) are small, metal-ion binding proteins (typically between 45 and 85 amino acids) that appear to be ubiquitous in eukaryotes and cyanobacteria. Several highly divergent MTs have been identified in cyanobacteria, protist algae, and higher plants. These MTs differ dramatically from mammalian MTs in amino acid sequences, charge, total cysteine content, cysteine spacing patterns, and length of linker domains. In particular, higher plants have moderately large, complex MT gene families, in contrast to the small, much less complex families found in mammals. The plant and algal MTs exhibit beneficial metal binding and induction properties that may protect these organisms from elevated levels of both toxic cadmium (Cd), mercury (Hg) and arsenic (As) and affect the homeostasis of nutrient metals like copper (Cu) and zinc (Zn). For example, in the marine brown algae *Fucus vesiculosus*, a 67-amino acid MT with 16 cysteine residues was found to be copper-inducible and bound both Cd (II) and Cu(II) in vitro. A pea class-2 MT increased copper tolerance and accumulation, when overexpressed in *Escherichia coli* and transgenic Arabidopsis, but did not affect levels of Zn and Cd (Evans *et al.*, 1992). Previously, more than eight MT genes in four sequence classes have been described in Arabidopsis (Cobbett 2000).

Despite animal MTs being among the first genes expressed in transgenic plants , little is known about the functions of the various plant MT sequences themselves or why there is so much sequence diversity.

Introduction of mammalian MT gene into *B. compestris, B. napus* and *N. tabacum* confers Cd tolerance by increasing complexation of metal with MT and minimizing translocation of Cd to the shoots (Cobbett, 2000; Zimeri *et al.*, 2005). A number of genes in plants have been found to encode MT-like proteins having seqnence similarity to animal MT proteins. A number of MT-encoding genes were identified *in Arabidopsis.* A total of eight genes constitute MT-gene family in

Arabidopsis (Zhou and Goldsbrough, 1994). MTs have highest complexing affinity for Cu and are induced by exposure to it (Murphy *et al.*, 1997). On Cu treatment, strong induction in MT2 mRNA level has been observed *in Arabidopsis*. When genes for MT 1 and MT2 from *Arabidopsis* were expressed in an MT-deficient yeast mutant, both genes complemented the mutation and provided a high level of resistance to Cu (Zhou and Goldsbrough, 1994). Similarly, in Cu-sensitive mutants *of Arabidiopsis* it was shown that MT genes could be induced by Cu. There appears to be similarity between MTs and PCS for complexation with metals as observed in plants such as datura and maize (Rival et *al.*, 1990). The role of MTs as antioxidants has also been advocated (Wong *et al.*, 2004). A decrease in MT levels could result in increased level of free transition metal ions (Briat, 2002). According to Wong *et al* (2004) a rice metallothionein protein OsMT2b appears to function as an ROS scavenger, which depicts the antioxidative role of plant metallothioneins. Similarly, NO-scavenging capacity and involvement in plasma membrane repair appear to be additional roles of MTs (Salt *et al.*, 1998).

Detoxification of Metals by Organic acids and Amino acids

An alternative approach for detoxification of metals involves formation of metals-organic acid or metal-amino acid complexes in many plant species. A wide range of metals, viz., Cd, Pb, Ni, Mn and Al are either partially or in certain cases completely detoxified by this way. Plants are protected from the toxic effects of Ni in their tissues by its complexation with the anions of hydrocarboxylic acids such as citrate, malate and malonate (Clemens, 2001; Jocsak *et al.*, 2005; Mishra and Dubey, 2006) and the amino acid histidine (Kramer *et al.*, 1996). Generally, the coordination complexes formed by heavy metals with exclusively oxygen-donor centers do not have especially high stability constants, whereas histidine acts as a tridentate ligand, at typical cytoplasniic pH values, with its two nitrogen and one oxygen-donor centers and is therefore more efficient and selective chelator of heavy metal Ni than the hydroxycarboxylic acids. Complexation of Ni with another high affinity ligand, nicotinamine, has also been reported (Vacchina *et al.*, 2003). In non-polluted soils, Cd usually gets complexed with vacuolar citrate and when Cd concentration rises PC plays a crucial role (Wagner, 1993). Cd and Zn resistance of *Atriplex halimus* L. is due to precipitation of metals in oxalate crystals (Lutts *et al.*, 2004). In *Oryza sativa* L. synthesis of oxalate represents a significant response mechanism that enhances tolerance to Pb (Yang *et al.*, 2000).

Organic acid mediated detoxification is an important strategy adopted by plants to reduce Al toxicity. Organic acids chelate with Al and reduce its toxic effects at the cellular level (Ma, 2000). The complexes of Al-citrate (1:1) in hydrangea and Al-oxalate (1:3) in buckwheat have been well characterized (Ma, 2000). Little is known about the way by which Al-organic acid complexes are transported across membranes but it is likely that specific transporters are involved. Chelation of metals with ligands such as histidine, citrate, etc. helps in routing them primarily to the xylem (Kramer *et al.*, 1996; Salt and Kramer, 2000; Hall, 2002).

Antioxidative Defense Mechanism

Heavy metals increased the formation of reactive oxygen species (ROS) and results into oxidative stress and causes oxidative damage to biomolecules such as lipids, proteins, nucleic acids etc. (Dubey and Mishra, 2006; Panda and Matsumoto, 2007, Panda, 2008; Tiwari *et al.*, 2008). In general these ROS (O_2 , OH and H_2O_2) are products of normal cellular metabolism, their production is under tight control due to cellular antioxidative defense system. Induction in the activities of antioxidative enzymes as well as increase in the level of non-enzymic antioxidants are the strategies adopted by plants to scavenge ROS and to reduce oxidative damage caused due to ROS under heavy metal stress (Mishra and Dubey, 2006; Panda and Matsumoto, 2007; Panda, 2008). Recent reports suggest that though antioxidative defense system is not directly involved in heavy metal detoxification yet ROS play important role as intermediate signaling molecules to regulate the expression of genes for plant's defense system (Mishra and Dubey, 2006; Panda 2008, Tiwari *et al.*, 2008).

Heavy metal sequestration in vacuoles

Vacuolar sequestration of a number of heavy metals like Cd, Ni, As, Zn is known which diverts metal ions from metabolically active compartments (cytosol, chioroplasts, mitochondria) and minimizes the harmful effects of metal ions to vital cellular processes. Transporters are present in internal membranes to allow regulation of stored metals in organelles. Active accumulation of most of the metal ions is driven by the electrocheniical potential by electrogenic proton influxes *via* the vacuoler W-ATPase. Cd is transported across the tonoplast by a Cd_2/H antiport mechanism. Both vacuolar and extravacuolar localization of Ni ion occurs via a pH-gradient dependent manner in yeast whereas in Ni-hyperaccumulator plant *Thalspi goesingense* vacuolar metal transport proteins termed as metal-tolerance proteins (TgMTPs) are involved in compartmentalization of Ni in vacuoles in shoots (Persans *et al.*, 2001). Arsenic is also primarily stored in the vacuoles. Transport of Zn to the vacuole is mediated by 'Zn-malate shuttle'; malate being liberated in exchange for oxalate or citrate and is shuffled back to cytoplasm (Ernst *et al.*, 1992) but the storage form of Zn in the vacuoles is not much studied. A gene *(ZAI)* closely related to animal ZnT (Zn transporter) gene has been isolated from *Arabidopsis*. Overexpression of ZAT gene in transgenic plants led to enhanced accumulation of Zn in the roots under high Zn treatment.

Within plant cells, PC-metal complexes bound by GSH or PCs are shuttled to the vacuole by an ABC-type transporter protein in the tonoplast . The same type of transporter is involved in shuttling GSH-conjugated anthocyanins to the vacuole . In fact, anthocyanins can also bind metals , and have been suggested to play a role in metal sequestration. Other metal-binding molecules that are involved in metal complexation in the vacuole are organic acids . To date, the best characterized of the known vacuolar transporters and channel involved in metal tolerance is YCF1 from Saccharomyces cerevisiae. YCF1 is an MgATP energized glutathione S-conjugate transporter responsible for vacuolar sequestration of organic compounds after their S-conjugation with glutathione, as well as GSH metal complexes. It catalyzes the transport of bis (glutathionate) cadmium (Cd-GS2) into vacuoles , as well as As-GS3 and Hg-GS2 (Yang et al., 2005; Mishra and Dubey, 2006).

Conclusion and future perspective

In the past few years we have seen tremendous progress in our molecular understanding of plant tolerance of heavy metals, namely Cd, Cu, Zn, Al, As..etc. Much less is known about tolerance of metals such as lead or mercury. There is also some insight now into the molecular nature of entry pathways for Cd^{2+} and $AsO_4{}^{3-}$. However, detailed and quantitative understanding of various metal accumulation in plants is lacking particularly in mycorrhizal plants/systems. The actual contribution of uptake systems under different environmental conditions (soil pH, micronutrient supply etc.) or the location and structure of metal–ligand complexes are mysterious. The same is true for the molecular mechanisms underlying the considerable diversity found among crop plants with respect to metal detoxification. Finding the responsible genes will be important because low metal content of edible plant parts might well become a target of future crop breeding programs. There are some direct or indirect evidences now for plant responses specifically to the presence of non-essential toxic metals but detail understanding of the sensing of heavy metal exposure and the signaling cascades leading to respective transcriptional responses is lacking. Further, the molecular dissection of a suitable and specific marker response to heavy metal exposure using genomic, proteomic tools along with other advanced molecular techniques can add better understanding of heavy metal detoxification of plant in future.

References

1. Azevedo, J. A. and Azevedo, R. A . 2006. Heavy metals and oxidative stress: where do we go from here? *Communication in Biometry and Crop Science.* **1 (2)**: 135-138.

2. Benavides, M. P., Gallego, S. M. and Tomaro, M. L. 2005. Cadmium toxicity in plants. *Brazillian. Journal of Plant Physiology.* **17**: 21-34.

3. Clemens, S. 2001) Molecular mechanism of plant metal tolerance and homeostasis – *Planta* **212**: 475 – 486.

4. Cobbett, C. S. 2000. Phytochelatins and their role in heavy metal detoxification. Plant Physiol. **123**: 825 – 883.

5. Ernst, W. H. O., Krauss, G. J., Verkleij, J. A. C. and Wesenberg, D. 2008. Interaction of heavy metals with the sulphur metabolism in angiosperms from an ecological point of view. *Plant Cell and Environment.* **31**: 123–143.

6. Ernst, W. H. O., Verkleij, J. A. C. and Schat, H. 1992. Metal tolerance in plants – Acta Bot. Nerr. **41**: 229 – 248.

7. Evans, N. H., McAinsh, M. R., Hetherington, A. M., Knight and M. R. 2005. ROS perception in *Arabidopsis thaliana*: the ozone induced calcium response. *Plant Journal.* **41**: 615–626.

8. Gallego, S.M., Benavides, M. P. and Tomaro, M. L. 1996. Effect of heavy metal ion excess on sunflower leaves: evidence for involvement of oxidative stress, Plant Sci., **121**,151 – 159.

9. Goldsbrough, P. 2000. Metal tolerance in plants: the role of phytochelatins and metallothiones – In: Terry, N., Banuelos, G. (ed) Phytoremedation of contaminated soil and water. Pp. 221 – 233, CRC Press, LLC.

10. Gratão, P. L, Polle, A., Lea, P. J. and Azevedo, R. A. 2005. Making the life of heavy metal-stressed plants a little easier. *Functional Plant Biology* **32**: 481-494.

11. Grill, E, Winnacker, E.,L and Zenk, M. H. 1985. Phytochelatins: the principal heavy-metal complexing peptides of higher plants. *Science* **230**: 674- 676

12. Grill, E., Loffler, S., Winnacker, E. L. and Zenk, M. H. 1989. Phytochelatins, the heavy metal binding peptides of plants are synthesized from glutathione by a specific g - glutamyl cystein dipeptidyl transpeptidase (phytochelatin synthase) – *Proc. Nat. Acad. Sci., USA* **86**: 6838 – 6842.

13. Hall, J. L. and Williams, L.E. 2003. Transition metal transporters in plants. *Journal of Experimental Botany* **54**: 2601–2613

14. Hall, J. L. 2002. Cellular mechanism of heavy metal detoxification and tolerance – *J. Exp. Bot.* **53(366):** 1 – 11.

15. Jócsák, I., Végvári, G. and Droppa, M. 2005. Heavy metal detoxification by organic acids in barley seedlings. *Acta Biologica Szegediensis* **49(1-2)**: 99-101.

16. Jonak, C., Nakagami, H. and Hirt, H. 2004. Heavy Metal Stress. Activation of Distinct Mitogen-Activated Protein Kinase Pathways by Copper and Cadmium. *Plant Physiology* **136** : 3276–3283.

17. Kramer, U., Cotter – Howells, J.D., Charnock, J. M., Baker, A. J. M. and Smith, A.C. 1996. Free histidine as a metal chelators in plants that accumulate nickel – *Nature* **379**: 635 – 638.

18. Ma, L.Q., Komar, K. M., Tu, C., Zhang, W., Cai, Y. and Kennelly, E. D. 2001. A fern that hyperaccumulates arsenic. *Nature* **409**:579.

19. Maitani, T., Kubota, H., Sato, K. and Yamada, T. 1996. The Composition of Metals Bound to Class III Metallothionein (Phytochelatin and Its Desglycyl Peptide) Induced by Various Metals in Root Cultures of Rubia tinctorum. *Plant Physiology*, **110** : 1145–1150.

20. Mishra, S. and Dubey, R. S. 2006. Heavy metal uptake and detoxification mechanisms in plants. Int J.Agri. Res **1(2)**:122-141.

21. Murphy, A. S., Eisinger, W. R., Shaff, J. E., Kochian, L.V. and Taiz, L. 1999. Early copper induced leakage of K^+ from *Arabidopsis* seedlings is mediated by ion channels and ccoupled to citrate efflux. *Plant Physiol.* **121**: 1375 – 1382.

22. Pal, R. and Rai, J. P. N. 2009. Phytochelatins: Peptides

Involved in Heavy Metal Detoxification. *Applied Biochemistry Biotechnology*. DOI. 10.1007/s12010-009-8565-4

23. Panda, S. K. 2008. Impact of copper on reactive oxygen species, lipid peroxidation and antioxidants in *Lemna minor*. *Biologia Plantarum* **52** **(3)**: 561-564.

24. Panda, S. K. and Patra, H. K. 1997. Physiology of chromium toxicity. A review; Plant *Physiol Biochem*. **24**, 10—17.

25. Panda, S. K., Chaodhury, I. and Khan, M. H. 2003. Heavy metal phytotoxicity induces lipid peroxidation and affect antioxidants in wheat leaves. *Biol. Plant.* **46**: 289-294.

26. Panda, S. K. and Choudhury, S. 2005. Chromium stress in plants. *Braz. J. Plant Physiol.* **17(1)**: 95-102.

27. Panda, S. K. 2007. Chromium mediated oxidative stress and ultrastructural changes in root cells of developing rice seedlings. *J. Plant Physiol.* , **164** **(11)**:1419-1428.

28. Salt, D.E., Blaylock, M., Kumar, P. B. N., Dushenkov, E., Ensley, B. B., Chet, I. and Raskin, I.. 1995. Phytoremedation: A noble strategy for the removal of toxic metals from the environment using plants. - *Biotechnology* **13**: 468 - 474.

29. Sanita di Toppi L, Prasad, M. N. V. and Ottonello, S. 2002.. Metal chelating peptides and proteins in plants. In: Prasad MNV, Strzaka K (ed) Physiology and Biochemistry of heavy metal detoxification and tolerance in plants. Kluwer Academic Publishers, Dordrecht, The Netherlands, pp 59 - 93.

30. Shanker, T., Cervantes, C., Loza-Taverac, H. and Avudainayagamd, S. **2005.** Chromium toxicity in plants. *Environment International* **31**: 739- 753

31. Sharma, R. K., Agrawal, M. and Agarwall, S. B. 2008. Interactive Effects of Cadmium and Zinc on Carrots: Growth and Biomass Accumulation. . *Journal of Plant Nutrition* **31**: 19–34.

32. Tewari, R. K., Kumar, P. and Sharma, P. N. 2006. Antioxidant responses to enhanced generation of superoxide anion radical and hydrogen peroxide in the copper-stressed mulberry plants. *Planta* **223**: 1145–1153.

33. Wagner, G. J. 1993. Accumulation of cadmium in crop plants and its consequences to human health. *Advances in Agronomy* **51**:173 212

34. Xiang, C. and Oliver, D. 1998. Glutathione metabolic genes coordinately respond to heavy metals and jasmonic acid in Arabidopsis. *Plant Cell* . **10**: 1539-1550.

35. Yang, X., Fenga, Y., Hea, Z. and Stofella, P. J. 2005. Molecular mechanisms of heavy metal hyperaccumulation and phytoremediation. *Journal of Trace Elements in Medicine and Biology* **18** : 339–353.

36. Zhang, H., Xia, Y., Wang, G. and Shen, Z. .2008. Excess copper induces accumulation of hydrogen peroxide and increases lipid peroxidation and total activity of copper–zinc superoxide dismutase in roots of *Elsholtzia haichowensis*. *Planta* **227**: 465–475.

37. Zhou, J. and Goldsbrough, P.B. 1994. Functional homologues of fungal metallothionein gene from *Arabidopsis*. *Plant Cell*. **6**:875-884

Author Index

Subject Index